PRAISE FOR THE BIOLOGY OF BUSINESS

Why We Should Treat Our Businesses Like Our Bodies

When all of the human body's organs and systems are working well, we all have the expectation of certain performances from being in that healthy state. Christopher's body of work (pun intended), The Biology of Business shows us how the effort to create and support a healthy "Business" body gives rise to more formal performances that we typically expect from most business operations. Christopher has unlocked and translated how this biological connection directly correlates to the way businesses thrive or die. The idea that We "Should Treat Our Businesses Like Our Bodies" leads to the natural or biological consequence of this body of work, an exponential increment in the bottom line.

Mike Whitehead
CEO/Founder, Center for Intentional Leadership

I enjoyed reading The Biology of Business. The message throughout, that a healthy or diseased business has strong analogies to the similar conditions in the human body (with excellent examples of specific organ systems), is a clever means of simplifying a complex relationship. Dr. Eaddy points out that businesses, like life, can ultimately come to an end often due to lack of insight, adaptability, novel technological advances, and competition. Although the human form inevitably ends, the lost life leaves a legacy (DNA) for future generations. Thank you for adding this well thought authoring to the written record.

WVU Radiation Oncology Division
Jondavid Pollock, MD, PhD, Director

The Biology of Business masterfully bridges the gap between biology and organizational development, presenting a compelling case for viewing businesses as living organisms. Eaddy's insightful comparisons will resonate deeply with those who see organizations as interconnected systems, thriving only through growth, adaptation, and holistic health. This book is a must-read for anyone passionate about organizational development.

Gerald Lackey Commissioner of the
Virginia Department of Motor Vehicles

THE BIOLOGY OF BUSINESS

Why We Should Treat Our Businesses Like Our Bodies

CHRISTOPHER L EADDY

Contributions by: Robin Bittner and
Collin Christopher Eaddy

The Biology of Business
© Copyright <<2024>> Christopher L Eaddy

ISBN: 979-8-9987104-0-7 - paperback
ISBN: 979-8-89109-113-9 - ebook

TABLE OF CONTENTS

Foreword vii

Note from the Author xi

Prelude. xv

Introduction xix

Chapter One: Every Organism Either Grows or Dies 1

Chapter Two: The Anatomy Comparison. 9

Chapter Three: The Heart and Lungs
The Core Elements of Business Reconsidered 27

Chapter Four: Disease. 37

Chapter Five: The Impact of Aging on Human
Organisms and Organizations. 55

Chapter Six: A Conversation Between a Coroner
and an Organizational Health Consultant 68

Chapter Seven: Concepts To Execution
(What We've Gained From our Learning Journey) 80

Chapter Eight: Remediation and Rehabilitation—
How Biology Thrives 92

Thought Leadership: Gateways to
Enhanced Mindfulness. 109

Gratitude. 141

References 145

FOREWORD

In writing *The Biology of Business*, I pursued the exploration of the intricate parallels between the biological systems that govern our bodies and the systems that drive successful businesses. To bring a unique perspective to this idea, I invited Dr. Jondavid Pollock, a distinguished medical professional, to share insights as a reader/listener of the *Biology of Business* through the filters of medicine that resonate with the principles discussed in this book.

Dr. Pollock is renowned with more than 25 years of experience in oncological radiology. With a deep understanding of the human body's inner workings, Dr. Pollock has seen firsthand how biological principles can inform and inspire innovation beyond the realm of medicine.

I am honored to share a letter from Dr. Pollock that beautifully encapsulates the central theme of this book. In this letter, he draws on his medical expertise to highlight the importance of viewing our businesses through a biological lens, emphasizing the significance of nurturing and sustaining organizational health.

Dear Readers,

As a medical professional, I have spent my career observing the complex yet remarkably efficient systems that govern the human body. I am delighted to see a book like The Biology of Business *that recognizes the profound lessons these systems can teach us about maintaining healthy and thriving organizations...*

WVU Cancer Institute

Cancer.org

Radiation Oncology Division
Jondavid Pollock, MD, PhD, Director
1 Medical Park
Wheeling, WV 26003
Phone / 304-243-3490

I enjoyed reading The Biology of Business and learned quite a bit, both about business (the specific examples from the corporate world were very helpful) and what appears to be Dr. Eaddy's excellent grasp of the psychology behind business systems. As the director of my division, a senior physician at the hospital where my experience is often requested regarding patient throughput, improving efficiencies, calling out bad actors (via a peer review process), and giving advice to young leaders who are trying to optimize their own leadership efforts, I found the author's examples helpful, succinct, and thoughtful. The message throughout, that a healthy or diseased business has strong analogies to the similar conditions in the human body (with excellent examples of specific organ systems), is a clever means of simplifying a complex relationship. Perhaps the most relevant analogy he drew is the need for transparency as "it always comes across as authentic". Signs of a body's failure, manifest by symptoms, should not be ignored as they herald preventable conditions that left untreated or addressed, can lead to far greater problems and even death. Identifying avoidable problems will certainly improve a body's performance, quality of life, and longevity and I suspect, as the author has ably addressed in this book, can help direct a business toward a successful life span. Interestingly Dr. Eaddy points out that businesses, like life, can ultimately come to an end often due to lack of insight, adaptability, novel technological advances, and competition. Although the human form inevitably ends, the lost life leaves a legacy (DNA) for future generations. Similarly, even when a specific business ends, its history (both its successes and failures) serve as an algorithm to a future generation.

I am deeply grateful to Dr. Jondavid Pollock for his thoughtful contribution, which provides a compelling bridge between the fields of biology and business. I hope that this foreword, along with Dr. Pollocks insights, will inspire you to look at your organization in a new light—as a living, breathing entity that requires careful nurturing and strategic care.

Wishing you health,

Dr. Christopher Eaddy
Author of *The Biology of Business: Why We Should Treat Our Business Like Our Bodies*

NOTE FROM THE AUTHOR

I was a consultant at the time I began thinking about this book, working with a global interest client. I was listening to an executive speak to a group of employees one evening, when someone asked, "What resource books and readings do you find to be motivational and inspirational?" The executive's answer was surprising: "I don't read a lot of books," he said. "I find that most of them take too long to get to the point."

This statement stuck with me, and I decided to author a book that would get straight to the point.

Inspired by working in the medical field (Emergency Department [ED]) and information learned in nursing school (anatomy and physiology), I recall the moment the reality of immortality struck me. One evening, while working on the trauma team in the ED, I had to apply a sense of logic to what I normalized on a daily basis at WakeMed Hospital. Specifically, a young, active thirty-eight-year-old in distress was the precall to the hospital. "Possible stroke," echoed across the radio. Seven minutes later the paramedics arrived, and I was nearly shaken to my core to see a friend lying there suffering from a hypertension stroke. Despite all we did and could think to do, he died the next morning.

That was just one of the many startling sights of sad, unstoppable, unpreventable endings to life which unconsciously seemed to be a regular event. Equally important were the moments when I got to see many people brought back from the brink of complete pronouncement. Having familiarity with the mortuary sciences from extended family working in that field, I wasn't bothered by much of what I experienced on my nights and weekend shift. It seemed to almost be commonplace with me—death, that is. I ventured one day and read *How We Die* by Sherman B. Nuland, a Pulitzer Prize–winning surgeon, a great read simply out of curiosity and work relevance. However, it was the spark that years later would lead to this book.

With that health background, a psychologist's understanding of change and people as well as an engineer's training in serial thinking, I began thinking about my experiences in business, government, construction, technology, education and being a servant leader over thirty years, asking myself what had I learned and if there is a connection between it all—and if so, what was it? The simplicity of what I arrived at was not simple but amazing, as it would prove to be something that every person who reads this book can relate to, that is themselves as human organisms.

There are some scientific principles related to living organisms that ring true and are consistent in comparison to business organizations. They are enigmatic of what or who and when.

It starts with a simple premise, "*Organisms* either are living or they are dead." In most cases, *Organizations,* that live well, show up as exceptional in their field, some are dying as we read and others still, are barely living.

Another way to look at this or understand it in this context is to think about it in terms of "every living thing, including organizations, either grow or die." This takes into account adaptations of businesses, which have no limited capacity of lifespan, perhaps the only entity from the *origin*, from the word *organ* (Latin: organic or natural, refers to something living), which can survive for as long as humans exist.

PRELUDE

In business, it's often said that the fastest way from point A to point B is a straight line. Whether true or not, this book follows that strategy and gets right to the point. The main premise is that businesses are like living organisms, and if they don't adapt to changing conditions, they will die. The author uses his background from nursing school, engineering classes, psychology, practical corporate and business experiences, as well as years of developing programs that enhance team dynamics, consulting, and government experience, to draw comparisons between the life cycle of businesses (organizations) and the life cycle of living organisms.

The book begins by drawing comparisons between the human body and a business organization. Both are made up of cells and tissues that perform specific functions, and both have a signaling mechanism to identify problems and find solutions. The author argues that businesses, like human beings, are living organisms that either grow or die. At some point in their growth, businesses reach a point of maturity where their usefulness peaks, and they begin to decline. That is unless they understand the ways businesses die and what to do to overcome the issues that cause the ailments that lead to business death.

The author identifies five ways that living organisms, including businesses, can die: heart failure, respiratory failure, organ failure, cell death, and brain death. Each of these ways can be applied to businesses, and the author shows how they can be identified and addressed before it's too late. For example, heart failure in a business can occur when it loses its core customers and the culture across the company does not know how to realign and regain market share. Respiratory failure can occur when an organization fails to adapt to changing market conditions and "breathing-living" becomes difficult. This is normally brought on by not having a learning culture; screening in good air while creating vibrance in the organization.

To illustrate his point, the author provides real-world examples of businesses that failed to adapt to changing market conditions or other warning signs. Blockbuster was a video rental chain that was once the leader in its industry. However, when online streaming services like Netflix emerged, Blockbuster failed to adapt and eventually went bankrupt trying to "keep up." This example shows how important it is for businesses to recognize when their usefulness is declining and make the necessary changes to stay relevant.

The book concludes by emphasizing the importance of paying attention to the symptoms of decline in a business and taking action to address them. The author argues that businesses, like living organisms, require constant attention and care to remain healthy and vibrant. If they are neglected, they will eventually die. The book offers practical advice on how to identify the symptoms of decline and what to do, to course correct them.

At its core, this book is about providing managers and leaders with a new perspective on organizational structures and systems and how they can be optimized for maximum efficiency and effectiveness. By drawing on the natural structures and systems of the human body, the author hopes to provide readers with valuable insights and strategies for achieving their full potential and promoting the long-term health and success of their organizations.

Finally, if you are in a business at any level, and especially in leadership, this book is a must-read if you want to stay ahead of the constant curves. The author's comparisons between living organisms and businesses provide a unique perspective on the challenges businesses face. The real-world examples throughout this book serve as cautionary tales for businesses that fail to adapt to changing conditions, demands, and adversity. The book's emphasis is on finally seeing what is really happening in your business and understanding what it means and how to prioritize fixing it. With really easy-to-grasp pathways to solutions, this book gives quite practical advice for anyone looking to keep their business healthy and vibrant.

INTRODUCTION

As she reflected on the journey that had brought her to this point, she realized that without this book—its mindset and actionable steps—her organization would not have transitioned successfully into the post-pandemic era. In this new landscape, business now encompasses AI, inclusion efforts, economic tension relief, remote and faster-paced work environments, clarity in customer demand, uninterrupted value flow, competitive advantages, and strategies to bridge the gap between seasoned workers and a new generation of employees—many of whom have never set foot in an office. She also had to consider plans to manage global political instability. "The Biology of Business," she said, "saved my company's life."

As Sarah sat at her desk, a sense of unease washed over her. Her company had been struggling lately, and she was among the managers tasked with turning things around. Despite the considerable effort and resources dedicated to this endeavor, nothing seemed to be working.

Sarah began to wonder if there was something deeper at play—something beyond the surface-level issues they were attempting to address. She had attended countless training sessions and read numerous books on leadership, management, and organizational development, yet none seemed to provide a comprehensive solution to the challenges she faced. She needed a new perspective—a fresh way of thinking about the complex organism that was her organization. That's when she stumbled upon a book that would forever change her view on organizational management.

The book was called *"The Biology of Business: Why We Should Treat Our Businesses Like Our Bodies,"* and it was intriguing. Sarah began to read, and what she found was eye-opening.

The book drew parallels between the human body and organizations, highlighting that both are complex systems composed of different parts that must work together seamlessly to achieve success. The author argued that just as the human body can fall ill or even die due to various factors, organizations too can experience decline and failure.

It explored how disease and dysfunction in individual organs could impact the overall health of the human body, mirroring organizational dysfunction. The book offered strategies for addressing this dysfunction, including cultural training, information sharing, transparency, trust, innovation, structured capabilities, and a seamless flow of value to customers. Sarah realized these were precisely the strategies her organization needed to thrive.

But the book didn't just identify the problems; it also provided solutions. It emphasized the importance of culture, training, transparency, and leadership.

The book urged organizations to prioritize delivering value to customers without frustration. It discussed the importance of a strong organizational pulse and a learning culture, drawing parallels to the functions of the heart and lungs in the human body. It clearly illustrated that within any business ecosystem, culture serves as the primary domain of the organization, where the awareness of the need to coexist emerges first and learning accelerates the group's ability to progress swiftly.

Sarah couldn't put the book down. As she read on, she discovered the importance of transparency and trust within an organization, and how these elements could lead to innovation and structured capability development—a shift that many companies resist. She learned about the determinants of disease and dysfunction in individual organs and how these parallels could manifest as organizational dysfunction. The book even emphasized the significance of early detection and prevention of these issues, highlighting that innovation and adaptation are key to prolonging the health and success of an organization.

Sarah was amazed by the insights she gained from the book. It helped her better understand the complexities of her own organization and how she could contribute to its success. She couldn't believe how much the book resonated with her. She realized that her company had been so focused on fixing specific business issues that they had lost sight of the bigger picture. They had neglected to foster a culture of transparency and trust, as well as long-term partnerships with both customers and employees. This recognition ignited the initiative to turn her company around. It was the final piece she needed, clearly mapped out in *The Biology of Business*.

CHAPTER ONE

EVERY ORGANISM EITHER GROWS OR DIES

The journey began with a realization that continues to shake the core of human existence: every organism either grows or dies.

It started for me in the North Carolina governor's office, where I was overseeing a one-hundred-county initiative. As I embarked on my own journey of self-development in executive management, I dedicated my free time to writing curriculum for Tony Robbins' Discovery Camp for Leaders. Through this experience, I discovered a unique principle of human attributes: although my education suggested that our needs were based on a hierarchy stemming from Maslow and others, there exists another fundamental set of needs that most of us never learned about or discussed. These are the psychological needs: the need for connection, variety, certainty, contribution, and growth.

As humans, we have a psychological need for connection or love, which isn't always outward-facing. Some people may not thrive on human interaction but still require self-connection as a form of love. Love and connection are essential psychological needs.

Additionally, we require a sense of variety, which aligns with scientific theories of adaptation, nature versus nurture, and the survival of the fittest. Diversity, change, and variety are inherent to the human experience, but the ability to adapt and redirect is at the core of thriving. This is such an important aspect of business survival that it deserves special emphasis at the end of the chapter. This clarity will enhance our understanding of what it means to win, particularly in relation to healthy competition.

While diversity and variety are crucial psychological states, the same is true for certainty. This need for consistency is vital for the survival of nearly every living thing. It provides predictability in systems and operations, allowing for corrective actions when a system is out of alignment with itself.

The next two discoveries were profound, and even as a seasoned psychologist, I couldn't ignore their significant implications. The first was the idea that everything with good potential always seeks to share itself. This includes sunlight providing warmth, glaciers offering fresh water, trees producing clean air, and the Red Cross giving blood, assistance, and support for the betterment of others. As I worked to translate this idea to human behavior or that of an intelligent organism, I realized that we, as a species, have a fundamental need to contribute to one another. This psychological need is so ingrained in us that we often encounter stories of individuals sacrificing their own lives to save others—whether running into a burning building, jumping into a body of water, or helping someone defend themselves against a dangerous violent person. It is simply part of who we are.

The second discovery was the concept of growth. I first observed this phenomenon with tomatoes when I bought a new house with a spacious backyard in the southeastern United States, ideal for growing my own food. With blind enthusiasm and no guidance, I eagerly began tilling and preparing the large plot. My grand- parents were sharecroppers, so I thought that qualified me...I planted at least five types of vegetables, only to have them devoured at first bloom by rabbits and deer. After three unsuccessful attempts, I settled on tomatoes.

With minimal guidance, I planted them in a large container, placing it in a sunny spot and using stakes for support. As I watched impatiently almost daily, I noticed the first bloom, followed by the bud of an actual round baby tomato. It grew from the size of a quarter to that of a half-dollar coin and eventually reached the size of a baseball.

At first, there was the green ball, then the orange ball, and finally the fiery red tomato. In most cases, I managed to pick the tomatoes from the vine when they ripened. But then it happened. One day, I noticed a red tomato at the back of the stalky plant that I had missed. Too lazy at that moment and with more than enough already in the house, I opted to let it stay. It was ripe and had reached its peak.

When I returned to the plant about a week later, I pulled a few ripe tomatoes from it. I noticed that the one which had ripened a week ago had begun to wither. It had grown to its fullest potential and was no longer going to grow. In its state of withering, it was dying.

This realization extended beyond just plants. I began to observe the world around me: people dying, plants wilting in the heat, my parched lawn, roadkill, businesses closing, and parts of my organization being dissolved. It occurred to me:

The tomato was like all living things, organizations, and living organisms. If it was growing, it was living, and the moment it stopped growing, it was dying. And then another thought occurred: Organizations are perhaps the only living thing that can weather almost any calamity. As long as there are humans engaging in commerce, businesses can survive.

In light of those discoveries, I recalled the conversations I had with my PhD mentor, a former US Navy SEAL, with whom I traded workouts for mentoring during my coursework (the best worst decision I ever made). I remember how he consistently encouraged me during our twenty-six-mile bicycle rides, which I was not physically fit for, as well as the two-mile swims and two to five-mile runs that followed, along with other rigorous exercise routines. He would always say, "You got this. Adapt and overcome. You're strong, you will survive this. It's just a cramp. You're a human; you're built to overcome. It's in your genes." I survived, and the memories of nearly every workout remain vivid today. Those moments marked a time when I felt I had nothing left, yet he found a way to motivate me to push through.

Whether it was the environment, genetics, or simply the mindset of "there has to be a way to get through this," I later learned that the silent killer in business is our tendency to recognize the signs of struggle and possess the right mindset, yet employ the wrong tactics and strategies to address the issues. Understanding that these pitfalls can jeopardize your business leaves little room for hesitation if you want to survive.

The key to survival is action, especially if you want to turn things around now.

The importance of growth for businesses cannot be overstated. To survive and thrive in the ever-changing landscape of the business world, companies must continuously grow and adapt. This growth can take many forms, including expanding into new markets, developing new products or services, or improving existing processes. Companies that fail to grow and adapt will eventually become stagnant and ultimately perish.

One of the keys to successful growth is innovation. This involves finding new and creative ways to solve problems, meet customer needs, and stay ahead of the competition. Innovation can manifest in various ways, such as developing new technology, creating unique marketing strategies, or implementing novel business models.

Regardless of the form it takes, innovation is critical for businesses that aim to continue growing and thriving. We will also explore how to cultivate a culture that promotes cognitive diversity to ignite innovation—there is a way to maintain cohesion through shared core beliefs while benefiting from high levels of performance in execution. In other words, throughout this book, "pay attention to all things culture."

Another important factor in business growth is leadership. Strong leadership is essential for guiding a company through the ups and downs of the business world. Good leaders can inspire and motivate their teams, make tough decisions when necessary, and steer the company toward success. Without strong leadership, companies may struggle to adapt to changing market conditions and may ultimately fail.

Of course, growth also brings its own set of challenges. As companies expand and evolve, they may encounter issues such as increased competition, higher costs, and new regulatory requirements. Managing these challenges effectively requires careful planning, strategic thinking, and a willingness to take calculated risks.

I thought about the many businesses that had grown and then died, including TWA Airlines, Pan Am, Tower Records, Blockbuster Video, Woolworth, Parmalat, Compaq, Toshiba, Canadian Airlines, Eaton's, Nokia, MySpace, Commodore Corp, Polaroid, Kodak (Part I), Toys "R" Us, Enron, Comet, Kmart, and many more.

These businesses were once successful, but they failed to continue growing, and as a result, they perished. The same principle applies to individuals and organizations. If we stop growing, we start dying.

The tomato taught me a valuable lesson about growth and death: all living things either grow or die, and this principle holds true for businesses and individuals alike. We must continue to grow and evolve if we want to thrive and avoid stagnation and death.

"Adapt and overcome" is a popular phrase that's often used in military training, sports, and personal development. It is a mindset that employs courage and resilience. There is much science behind the hard-wired tendency toward resiliency in the human brain. It allows all humans to overcome obstacles and meet their objectives and desires.

An example where this phrase is used is in the US Marine Corps' Leadership Principles, where it says, "Be technically and tactically proficient. Know your job and your Marines. Seek responsibility and take responsibility for your actions. **Adapt to and overcome any obstacle.**"

REFERENCE:

- U.S. Marine Corps. (n.d.). Leadership Principles. Marines Leadership Principles

Nature versus nurture:

The nature versus nurture debate is older than most of us reading this, a psychology debate that has never ended, a debate of simply genetics versus environment. It is obvious that both play a role in human behavior, as we see in nature. (Why does a bear go to a campground? Genetically it is programmed to seek food, and environmentally it knows from experience, curiosity, or smell that people in campsites have food.) And yet we debate it. The identical twins argument has too many variables for anyone to ever prove whether environment or genetics influences the twins' decisions, because we cannot account for an infinity of variables.

REFERENCE:

- Plomin, R., DeFries, J. C., Knopik, V. S., & Neiderhiser,
- J. M. (2016). "Top 10 Replicated Findings from Behavioral Genetics." Perspectives on Psychological Science, 11(1), 3-23.
- Ridley, M. (2003). "Nature Via Nurture: Genes, Experience, and What Makes Us Human."

HarperCollins. (Flawed assumption they act independently."

○ Turkheimer, E. (2016). "Weak Genetic Explanation of Complex Traits Leads to Inflated Claims of Heritability." *Nature Human Behaviour*, 1(6), 0107. (overestimated claims).

○ Gottlieb, G. (1992). *Individual Development And Evolution: The Genesis of Novel Behavior.* Oxford University Press.

The strong survive:

"The strong survive" is often heard in the joke, "What happens if a bear comes after us? Do you think you can outrun it?" The response, "No, I just have to outrun you," implies that survival of the fittest may have earnest intentions, while perhaps the real strength is in the ability of a human to think—that ultimately implies innovation. Innovation is either unleashed in a company or it is squelched—I really don't think we needed Charles Darwin to tell us this. Evolution in companies is simple: Change or die. Using the collective knowledge of their employees is what makes surviving companies strong.

REFERENCE:

○ Thus Spoke Zarathusra—Nietzsche:

❑ The species that does not prevent itself from being destroyed will be destroyed; it is the inexorable logic of Nature. The strong are those who know how to take care of themselves; the strongest are those who know how to take care of themselves and others. This is easily translatable to business.

CHAPTER TWO

THE ANATOMY COMPARISON

Welcome to the fascinating world of the human body and its organs, where each part functions to keep the organism alive. In this chapter, we will explore the roles of different organs and compare them to a business organization.

My intention here is not to create a biology lesson, but it is imperative that we establish a synchronized understanding of how organs work to sustain the human organism. We will draw correlations right away and then delve into specific problems and concerns related to each organ and its corresponding business representation.

Shortly, it will make sense; this exploration will reinforce your understanding of what happens when these organs fail. It will help us grasp how such failures create a debilitating inability to function or even lead to death for both individuals and businesses.

Let's start with the brain. The brain is the control center of the human body, receiving stimuli and interpreting it. It then sends impulses to the body to react and respond to the stimuli, maintaining stability and creating balance when new conditions are presented. In a business organization, the CEO (president, senior partner, owner, etc.) or leader plays a similar role, absorbing information, interpreting it, and devising strategies to respond to challenges.

Next, consider the heart, which beats to maintain stability in a living system by moving blood rich in nutrients and oxygen. Similarly, a business organization needs a pulse or a sense of normalcy—to keep operations running smoothly. Any deviation from this pulse can indicate an issue that requires attention.

Now, let's turn to the lungs, which receive air, extract oxygen, and exhale carbon dioxide waste. In a business organization, this function can be likened to employees who take in information, analyze it, and release it in the form of valuable services and products. The lungs also have many applications, which we will explore in greater detail in the chapters ahead.

The liver is responsible for filtering blood from the digestive tract, detoxifying chemicals, and secreting bile. In a business organization, this function is akin to the financial department, which ensures the company's financial health and regulates the flow of money by receiving it, directing it where needed within the company, and providing guidance on how each area spends or consumes it. Another filter in business organizations is the management structure and hierarchy, which acts as a filter for the information that flows from the top.

While these are a few of the essential organs, other systems are also crucial to the body's functioning. The failure of any system or organ can significantly impact the entire organism, putting stress on other organs to compensate for deficiencies.

Similarly, in a business organization, any department that fails to perform at a high level can lead to significant repercussions, potentially putting the entire organization at risk. Therefore, it's crucial to pay attention to every aspect of the organization and ensure that each part is functioning optimally. Just as the kidneys filter blood and produce waste in the form of urine, the HR department plays a vital role in filtering out unsuitable candidates and fostering a productive workforce.

The eyes responsible for taking in stimuli, interpreting them, and responding accordingly, parallel the role of a customer service department.

The small intestine absorbs nutrients into the bloodstream, much like a marketing department that gathers information to create compelling marketing strategies. The small intestine's efforts are designed to help the entire system function at peak condition. Additionally, where the intestines cannot assimilate elements, they begin the process of creating waste for elimination—assimilation or elimination is a critical consideration for any system.

In business, there are also processes that foster assimilative behavior, such as dependencies, meetings, lines of communication, reporting structures, information-sharing methods, and performance evaluations. Feedback loops play a crucial role as well, providing insights into customer perceptions of your products and the overall quality of your services. These processes enable certain behaviors to become ingrained in the culture while others are discarded when they fail to yield results.

The small intestine absorbs nutrients into the bloodstream, much like a marketing department that gathers information to create compelling marketing strategies. The small intestine's efforts are aimed at helping the entire system function at peak condition. Additionally, when the intestines cannot assimilate certain elements, they initiate the process of creating waste for elimination— assimilation or elimination is a critical consideration for any system.

In business, there are also processes that companies use to foster assimilative behavior, such as dependencies, meetings, lines of communication, reporting structures, information-sharing methods, and performance evaluations. Feedback loops are essential as well, providing insights into customer perceptions of your products and the overall quality of your services. These processes enable certain behaviors to become ingrained in the culture while others are discarded when they fail to yield results.

Perhaps rephrasing it this way will make it clearer if it's not yet understood: the processes you implement in the system will either create a sense of normalcy or lead to difficulties in producing output (akin to waste in the body). Hot sauce in, hot sauce out. As for bad processes... well, you can safely assume the rest.

We must not overlook the skin and muscles (the integumentary system). They protect the body and enable movement, much like the legal and operations departments in a business organization, which safeguard the company and ensure it functions smoothly.

The human body and a business organization share many similarities. Both require every part to function optimally to maintain stability and peak performance. Any failure in any system or organ can significantly impact the entire organism or organization. Therefore, it is essential to pay attention to the various parts of the organization just as you do with your own body. Every aspect of the organization requires attention at some point. By addressing these needs, you ensure that each part is working together to achieve common goals.

In times of disease or attack, the body's systems must work in unison to respond effectively. Left to self-correct and heal on its own, there are three instances:

1. The rest of the body aids in healing the ailment, allowing it to become a functioning organ or system again.
2. The organ is either successfully removed or repaired, restoring its functionality.
3. It succumbs to its injury or disease, placing stress on other organs and ultimately burdening the entire system or organization.

Just as some organs require our attention, certain areas of our business need focus as well. Often, it's not the bottom line that demands the most attention. The heart, for example, plays a critical role in directing blood flow and disseminating information throughout the body, while the lungs are responsible for extracting oxygen from the air and expelling carbon dioxide waste. In a business context, the lungs symbolize the management of skills and training, among other aspects. They are also considered part of the cardiovascular system, highlighting how the heart and lungs work together and depend on each other.

The success of a company depends on the quality of its products or services and the efficiency with which they are produced. Just as the lungs efficiently capture oxygen for every cell in the body, effective training programs ensure that every employee possesses the skills and knowledge necessary to perform their job with excellence. This is the second most important aspect of turning a company around, as the lungs work in conjunction with the cardiovascular system to create optimal conditions—details we will cover later.

Reducing waste is crucial for optimizing efficiency and maximizing productivity. While companies may change policies or personnel, the most impactful waste reduction efforts often come from process improvements. Processes have clear structures and steps that can be optimized and streamlined to eliminate inefficiencies; in contrast, people have habits and mindsets that can be observed and influenced, but not easily changed.

Shared information and proactive opportunities for creating new ways of working (processes) are essential components of effective training and enablement programs (culture). By embracing these principles of growth and continuously seeking improvement, businesses can remain competitive and thrive in today's ever-changing economy and landscape of influential events.

The success of an organization heavily relies on its management structure, much like the liver, which filters blood and detoxifies chemicals in the body. The executives and management serve as the screening mechanism for the CEO's information sharing, filtering details to ensure they are clearly understood by employees for the long-term implementation of directives.

The triad of mental processing complexity, skills and talents, and values is essential for selecting the right people for management roles. If succession planning overlooks these three factors, it can lead to misguided employees, resulting in unfulfilled directives and broken strategies.

To put it bluntly: if you are a company leader or a manager overseeing team leads responsible for implementing product or service development that will take six months to a year, and it doesn't work, first examine your management structure. Instead of focusing on the people doing the work, consider the structure. Have you positioned them to succeed, or are you relying on a model you believe in that hasn't produced good results? As you will hear again, nothing changes until something moves.

The liver of the organization plays a crucial role in creating a pristine state of "blood," enabling the organization to resist foreign objects and detractors from the vision and strategy set forth by the brain. Requisite organization, also known as stratified systems theory (SST), is an effective succession planning method that ensures the right people are in the right place at the right time. Through this triad, it is evident that no one is suited for a management role without the proper skills, talents, and complexity of mental processing.

In addition to knowledge and skills, the company's values and the concept of "real work" are essential for executing strategy. These values must be reflected in the team, supporting their decisions and fostering innovation to gain market share or improve a product or service. The complexity of mental processing— the ability to think ahead— is crucial in decision-making. Carefully selecting management using the triad as a filtering mechanism ensures that employees are equipped to succeed.

This approach enables employees to respond effectively to the implementation of directives, leading to fulfilled objectives, self-organizing units, and a sense of value that employees take pride in creating and continuously delivering to customers.

A quick note on the triad: I had the privilege of working with Dr. Elliot Jacques, MD, PhD while at the NC Department of Justice—truly one of the most brilliant individuals I have ever known. Through PeopleFit, a company based in Raleigh, North Carolina, I met Dr. Jacques and had the opportunity to accompany him and the CEO of PeopleFit as they presented at the International Association of Chiefs of Police in Chicago one year. This association represents thousands of police chiefs from around the globe.

What I learned was straightforward, yet challenging to implement without guidance: no one is suited for a management role if they lack the appropriate work values, skills, talents, and complexity of mental processing (CMP). If you do not measure CMP upfront, you have only a slight chance of placing the right person in the right role. While it is possible to do this intuitively, it is neither the most efficient nor the most reliable method for hiring.

In considering biology and the natural state of work, Jacques' work as a medical doctor and psychoanalyst draws parallels between Human Resources as a system and the human body—what he terms "requisite organization," a natural HR system.

Let me explain the importance of the liver mechanism to an organism or system.

The triad mentioned earlier is not difficult to understand, yet it can be complex in its initial implementation. The simplest part of the process is to recognize that there are two components that are relatively easy to understand.

Knowledge and skills are somewhat self-explanatory; the ability to perform the job is either present or it is not. However, when it comes to values, the values Dr. Jacques refers to are not what we typically think of when considering values. This is largely true, as management is not only responsible for executing strategy but must also embody the values of the company and the concept of "real work."

These values are not about creation versus evolution or abortion versus the right to life. Rather, they pertain to the team dynamic. If the team decides a priority requires one more hour this week, will they support each other or abandon their colleagues? If the team proposes an innovation and wants to experiment to gain market share or improve a product or service, does the manager value that and create space for innovation, or do they operate from a command-and-control perspective, micromanaging and merely approving or disapproving work? This is what is meant by values.

Beyond knowledge and skills, which can be taught and learned, values are as personal as our individual breaths and can be flexible in the right situations. Complexity of mental processing, on the other hand, is entirely different and often unknown to most of us. It is the ability to think ahead and is biologically locked to our maturation. Here is an excerpt from an article about stratified systems theory and Elliott Jacques's work (1991):

> Jacques and his co-author, Clement, explain that a managerial leadership role requires an individual to organize, solve problems, and Managers must provide meaning for their subordinates, which requires the capability to see further than the individuals they are leading. Otherwise, they will fail to add value to their employees. The challenge lies in identifying conditions where the manager's capabilities can positively impact the organization's performance, as well as finding an accurate measure of an individual's capability for the role in which they serve.

And from the *Harvard Business Review*:

> Hierarchy is not to blame for our problems. The reason we have a hierarchical organization of work is not only that tasks occur at varying degrees of complexity—which is obvious— but also that there are sharp discontinuities in complexity that separate tasks into a series of steps or categories, which is less obvious.

There is no denying that hierarchical structures have been the source of considerable trouble and inefficiency. Their misuse has hampered effective management and stifled leadership, and their track record as a support for entrepreneurial energy has been far from exemplary. We might say that successful businesses have had to thrive despite hierarchical organization rather than because of it.

I think it is worthy of a marquee moment, reiterating what Jaques concluded with the immense data behind his work:

Managers **must** provide meaning for their subordinates, which requires the capability to see further than the individuals they are leading. Otherwise, they will fail to add value to their employees.

This is a critical basis for why any person in leadership (supervising others) must be accurately suited for their role. In the event that a manager, supervisor does not add value to their employees – they will get pulled into the weeds. This implies that a worker with *#* CMP and is matched to a role requiring at least that level of CMP, will be thinking the same thing their manager will be thinking when it comes to solutions. The manager (with no more than *#* CMP) gets pulled into the weeds of the employees tasks and the employee receives no real guidance because they are similar in their Complexity of Mental Processing- they will think about the next step to complete the work (out in time) in remarkably similar ways and perhaps no further out in time than each other. Companies will never grow rapidly with mismatched CMP in leadership.

This is also a common complaint in pulse surveys, many "managers seem to add no real value to the work of their subordinates" as voiced in every statement except "My manager helps me grow," and is validated by the fact that the breakup value of many large corporations exceeds their share value.

This clearly illustrates how much value corporate structures typically overlook.

Managers can detract from their subsidiary businesses, yet few of us know exactly what managerial added value looks like as it occurs.

Many people also complain that our current hierarchies bring out the more negative aspects of human behavior, such as greed, insensitivity, careerism, and self-importance. These qualities have driven many behavioral scientists to seek cooperative, group-oriented, non-hierarchical organizational forms. But are these traits inevitable companions of hierarchy, or are they products of its misuse that would diminish if hierarchy were properly understood and structured?

This work represents the most accurate succession planning I have ever encountered, spanning over forty years of study across thirty countries and involving thirty thousand individuals—all interviewed to establish the foundational premises. The results were remarkable, with a reliability of .96. (Nearly everything you eat, drive, and use at home and at work is based on some level of research, which typically achieves a reliability of 80 percent.)

In other words, if I can successfully perform a task 80 percent of the time, I should anticipate getting a similar result each time according to some principles of scientific statistical analysis. (Of course we know experiencing the other 20% may have dire consequences.)

This means that nearly every action and reaction—including a range of human behaviors such as sales, food consumption, purchases, commuting routes, and more—should demonstrate high levels of consistency when a minimum reliability threshold of 80% percent is met.

Conversely, the higher the reliability, the more you can depend on that level of consistency. Of course, you would want Your repelling lines to have 100 percent reliability. In most cases, we consume food, drink water or other beverages, trust our vehicles, and cross bridges or drive on roads separated by a flat yellow line from oncoming traffic—all of which have much lower reliability percentages than Dr. Jacques's work.

I will spend considerable time in this book discussing the liver and its role in the corporate world. It can make or break your enterprise and requires more than just a search firm, board interview, or panel to select the right person. Failing to choose based on hard data will result in the continued presence of ineffective managers who lack strong people skills and the ability to listen or convey information in ways that resonate with employees. This screening should be the bare minimum when hiring managers, especially top-level executives, where their impact will be most significant.

Of course, the simplest reason to purposefully create your hierarchy is that leaders will hold executives and managers accountable for the work of their subordinates. If they lack a clear CMP or do not understand the value of people and how to influence them, this will inevitably become a sore spot, causing ongoing grief and concern. Remember the triad.

Now, let's address the proverbial elephant in the room. If this succession planning is so reliable and valid, why haven't we heard more about it? In my opinion, the number one reason is that very few people understand how it is done. Those who do possess the expertise to conduct highly specialized interviews that yield results based on scientific biological maturation rather than personality alone. This means they can identify who to hire, who to prepare, and approximately when they may be ready for certain roles. Yes, it is predictive. It is based on a recorded interview session that is analyzed for specific markers indicating how far in advance a person can think and plan, their fitness for a particular role through their language patterns, and their stage of biological maturation. These language patterns reflect how individuals organize their thoughts when considering tasks or work specifically. The phrase "people are what they are" emerged from attempts to disprove this work; we found it incredibly difficult, even with practice, to deceive the interview process.

Again, people either have the CMP for a role or they don't. Roles in your company would be categorized in alignment with Jacques's stratums of requisite organization (stratified systems theory), with the requirements for each role determined ahead of the interviews. This gives you a 90-plus percent chance of selecting the right person, rather than just an above-average candidate who lacks the necessary CMP for the role.

Ultimately, the success of a company hinges on the quality of its products or services. It relies on the customer's perception of those offerings and the efficiency of production, ensuring that costs are minimized without negatively impacting quality or the willingness to sell (culture). These factors matter. In a business context, skill management and training are akin to the lungs of the organization, translating into the ability of workers to produce high-quality products and services.

One way to achieve this efficiency is to swiftly create the products customers want and maximize the time spent on any end-to-end effort, thereby reducing waste.

The lungs are not only proficient at capturing the oxygen needed for every cell in the body—similar to how training operates within a company at all task levels and for all roles—but they also expel waste. This expulsion of waste (carbon dioxide) symbolizes the adaptation of new ways of working, allowing inefficient practices to become a thing of the past. This is how information within a strategy becomes executable.

Although we typically want to focus more on our people during an economic downturn, we will always have processes in place to support employees. This is where we should often start to identify areas for improvement that facilitate transformation. (People have strengths and weaknesses; processes do not. Processes consist of structures and steps that either work or require improvements.) Admittedly, when circumstances change and processes become antiquated, they must either be completely overhauled or sunset and replaced with more efficient alternatives. In almost every instance, regardless of a company's overall performance, there are always processes that, when modified, can instantly improve the bottom line.

When it comes to addressing the challenges of gaining traction during times of change and concern, the easiest way to implement a strategy, change management plan, or transformation is to educate your employees. This is an often-overlooked principle of lean thinking and performance. The quickest way to change processes and behaviors is through shared information and opportunities for employees to proactively learn new skills, as well as practice and implement new ways of working. This forms the foundational value of all training and enablement. (learning culture) Of course, this all translates into rewards, recognition, and progress toward personal and corporate goals.

The benefits of changing and adapting to customer demands, validated trends, and opportunities—as well as human and technological advances—are crucial for company sustainability. They also provide the sustenance for which all employees work. Training fosters synchronicity, easily translating into momentum toward a common vision and facilitating both corporate and personal growth.

If we understand that training, like the lungs of a human, disseminates essential oxygen for maximizing life and existence, then the same holds true for businesses.

Training is the vehicle for spreading necessary information across the entire company, ensuring that needed changes and new ways of working take hold. Effective training becomes integrated into long-term behavior. As with most companies we choose to work for, it's important to remember, "We're in it together. We move together in any and all directions, through success and failure." This message must genuinely resonate from the leadership.

As a result of poor-performing managers, slow information sharing, and inadequate training to perform their tasks (think of the intestines, liver, and lungs), systems begin to fatigue, then cease to function, eventually creating stress on other parts of the organization. In some cases, the impact of one organ can lead to a complete shutdown of the entire organism.

An example of how this happens in organizations occurred when I was working with a U.S. company whose primary business was providing insurance policies. When certain software advancements emerged, it became the mission of the C-suite to stay current with the latest application offerings. In the haste and urgency of this transition, miscommunications and misunderstandings arose. Security was the last department to be informed of the upcoming changes. As the insurance company approached the promised completion deadline, they began advertising the launch. When the date arrived, they were instructed to proceed despite what they considered minor, fixable issues. A go/no-go meeting was held, and the lead manager stated, "We are more than ready to launch. Everyone who needs to know is informed—let's do it." This decision was supported by the majority of the managers. Unfortunately, there was no consultation with the manager overseeing the company's digital security. Within six months, a security breach occurred, costing the company millions of dollars to remediate.

Thirty percent of their workforce quit after the breach, they lost more than 75% of their customer base, and they are no longer in business under that name.

This situation clearly reflected a lack of leadership in management, poor information sharing, inadequate prioritization of important issues, an incomplete roadmap/timeline, and insufficient preparation of the security team for the impending changes. The failure of these systems prevented them from redefining new security protocols. This outcome could have been avoided if the company had understood its value proposition and how to uphold it, which certainly would have included security if there had been transparency, guidance, and effective communication. By the time they called for help, it was too late.

Over time, we can see that organizations operate like organisms in terms of systems. When these systems are nurtured and the organization's highest priority is the people who perform the work, it tends to function effectively. However, as we've seen, when any part of the system is neglected, Deming says it best: "A system will not look after itself." Ultimately, if left unmonitored, when challenges arise, unless the structure and management have fed the appropriate nutrients to the organ(s), these dysfunctions will stress other departments and can do so to a point of ultimately killing the body and any type of business.

CHAPTER THREE

THE HEART AND LUNGS
THE CORE ELEMENTS OF
BUSINESS RECONSIDERED

The human heart is a vital organ that pumps blood throughout the body, supplying organs and tissues with essential nutrients and oxygen. The heart's pulse measures its effectiveness in maintaining a healthy circulatory system. In a corporate organization, the heart and circulatory system represent the company's culture—the way employees at every level interact, communicate, and behave toward one another. A strong and healthy culture is essential for an organization's long-term success.

A company's culture is like a living, flowing, shapeable, and pulsating set of values, traditions, and ways of working. It shapes the habits of employees, and if left unattended, it can be influenced by strong personalities or arbitrary decision-makers, leading to poor leadership and a dysfunctional work environment. Therefore, it is crucial to cultivate a culture that aligns with the company's values, mission, and vision. A purposeful and intentional <u>culture</u> is more likely to lead to positive outcomes. In 'The Biology of Business,' we explore a key question: Does your company culture truly reflect its purpose? Many times, there's a big difference between what a company says its purpose is and what employees actually experience.

Culture is crucial in closing this gap and plays a big role in making a company's purpose and strategy real within the organization.

The heart and circulatory system are responsible for moving blood throughout the body but also removing waste. Similarly, a company's culture is responsible for creating an environment that fosters productivity, creativity, and innovation while removing barriers to growth and development. A healthy culture allows employees to perform to their optimal capabilities, leading to a thriving and successful organization.

In a company, the lungs represent the culture, pulse and leadership's direct impact. Leaders (by title) are responsible for disseminating information or strategy from the corporate leader to every employee in the organization. The direction the company takes is revealed through common beliefs, rumor dissolution, honesty, authenticity, and transparency. In a healthy organization, the CEO inspires employees to excel by being transparent and clear in their vision, which leads to employees finding meaning in their work.

The lungs work in tandem with the heart to ensure that every cell in the human organism receives the information it needs to perform optimally. Similarly, in an organization, the leadership must ensure that every employee has the information they need to perform their specific duties. Failure to disseminate information efficiently can lead to poor performance, negatively impacting individual cells, organs, and the entire system's ability to thrive.

Leadership is crucial to the success of any organization. The CEO is responsible not only for the bottom line but also for inspiring employees to excel. A charismatic, engaging, transparent, and clear CEO motivates employees to find meaning in their work and become more productive, fostering trust and autonomy. A healthy and robust culture requires regular waste removal and positive communication throughout the entire system. Employees derive purpose from the transparency, optimism, enthusiasm, and appreciation conveyed through information.

The culture of a company is like water, taking the path of least resistance and flowing to its lowest point. However, a purposeful and intentional culture is shaped by focused effort and a clear vision. This type of culture differs from that of living organisms, where cultures are often formed quietly and with less intent over time. The importance of deliberately shaping a business culture lies in the fact that organizations typically do not fail due to external pressures, but rather due to internal "disease"—the inability of systems to function well together and support each other's growth and stability.

One real-world example of a company that values a healthy culture is Google (ABC- stock symbol). The company's culture is built around transparency, open communication, and a focus on employees' well-being. Google's leadership emphasizes personal growth and discusses culture and personal development, recognizing that employee satisfaction and well-being are essential to the company's success. Google offers its employees a range of perks, such as on-site gyms, free meals, and flexible working hours to promote a healthy work-life balance. This approach has helped Google become one of the most successful and innovative companies in the world—its people!

The success of a company depends on the transparency of the information shared with employees and how well they understand and execute it. The more transparent and relevant the information, the more likely employees are to align with the company's vision, values, and goals. This kind of transparency fosters a company culture where employees understand their roles, are accountable for their work, and are engaged in the organization's success. When employees are motivated and engaged, they work more efficiently and productively, leading to the company's overall success.

The lungs are essential organs that extract oxygen from the air we breathe and distribute it to the organs and tissues through the bloodstream. Similarly, in a company, the lungs represent the information shared with employees, which is critical for creating a healthy and thriving work environment. This information equips employees with the knowledge needed to perform their tasks effectively, understand the company's mission, vision, and values, and be proactive in their roles. Healthy "lungs" ensure that employees know how they fit into the company structure and how their focused efforts can impact outcomes.

In smaller companies, the CEO or owner may be directly involved in tasks alongside employees, especially if they possess proprietary information, specialized skills, or licenses. Nonetheless, the CEO, president, leader, or owner still has a crucial role and responsibility within the company. As my first coaching client, a CFO of a large pharmaceutical company, once said, "Treat your employees as you would your customers." This means valuing and respecting employees, providing them with the tools and resources they need to perform their jobs well, and empowering them to contribute to the company's success.

In large corporate organizations, the management structure interprets information from the CEO—often seen as the brain—and passes it on to employees. This deep level of information is critical to the company's success and corresponds to the lower third of the lungs, where the richest and most dense air is found. However, when ego infiltrates the management structure, the information may become misaligned, leading to confusion, a lack of confidence and trust, and fear among employees. This fear, particularly the fear of losing their jobs for experimenting or being innovative, can be paralyzing and contribute to a company's decline.

A successful company culture is a learning culture. In such an environment, employees are eager to learn because they have discovered how they learn best, enabling them to work more efficiently and effectively. While this is a simple concept, it can be challenging to implement in a way that allows individuals to walk away from a single learning experience—be it a seminar, workshop, or training—having undergone a paradigm shift. This shift is both professional and personal, fostering an understanding of their true potential and their influence on excellence in their work.

Learning experts at companies like Rapid Change Group conduct these types of training sessions in just six hours with up to a hundred participants. They prioritize working with managers first, as this helps to eliminate ego and fear within the organization. (This is the "frozen layer," which we will discuss shortly.) In the absence of ego, desired outcomes typically emerge. In other words, the outcome takes precedence over ego, and companies that achieve this balance have a strong chance of weathering storms. Rapid Change Group collaborates with influencers and multipliers to infuse the culture with vigor and cultivate belief in the company's mission. They partner with executive leadership to take charge of the culture, shaping it into a flexible, responsive system that empowers leaders to guide the rest of the team.

The mission of companies like Rapid Change Group is to create resilient companies.

In any organization's culture, several critical elements must be accounted for in order for people to thrive. These include acknowledgment of the individual, clarity of purpose, direction, opportunities for learning, and acknowledgment that brings relief. Learning is an essential aspect of a company's culture, and the pursuit of knowledge and skills through active learning is vital for long-term success.

When these elements are lacking, an organization's competitive edge will begin to erode. The purpose of amplifying learning is to enable teams to move quickly and remain competitive. Therefore, it is essential to establish a learning environment and consider the specifics necessary for a company to stay ahead of its competitors.

When employees recognize their potential, they find meaning in their work more easily. The management structure effectively interprets information from the CEO—often viewed as the brain—providing employees with a launching point for what they need to know and learn. Conversely, in non-learning cultures, there is often a tendency for managers to engage in "people collecting" or headcount retention behavior, believing that having large numbers of employees equates to success. They may not embrace learning to improve their skills, and they may create an environment that discourages employees from wanting to learn and grow. This leads to stagnation in the company's growth.

Elliot Jacques's Requisite Organization (Stratified Systems Theory or SST) is a tool that can help you place the right person in the right role when it comes to management. Managers have a significant influence on culture, either allowing or prohibiting certain behaviors. The triad must be the focal point of any system transformation. Remember, the SST framework is based on knowledge and skills, values relevant to work situations, and the complexity of mental processing.

Employing this technique allows the pulse (heart) to consistently perform its functions with great results, contributing to the company's success.

The "frozen layer" refers to a situation where individuals at the top of an organization want to improve things, and those at the bottom want to grow and evolve, but the middle layer— middle management—is frozen and resistant to change. This layer needs rehabilitation, and it is crucial to gauge the pulse of employees who report to these managers. In a transparent ecosystem, it's essential to assess whether the manager can recover and redirect their efforts to align with the company's needs.

To illustrate the concept of the frozen layer, consider a software development company. The CEO wants to introduce new technologies to enhance the company's competitiveness, but middle management is resistant to change. They are comfortable with existing technologies and do not see the need for a shift.

This reluctance of people to supervise makes them appear valuable compared to performance. They may not embrace the idea of learning to improve their skills, and they may create an environment that discourages employees from wanting to grow. This ultimately leads to stagnation in the company's growth.

Again, the SST framework is based on knowledge and skills, values relevant to work situations, and the complexity of mental processing. Managers in the correct role where this technique is used to place them allows them to comfortably generate a healthy pulse (heart) and culture that consistently perform its functions effectively, contributing to the company's success.

Utilizing the stratified systems theory can help place the right people in the right roles, taking performance to the next level and driving the company's growth and achievement of goals. Ultimately, regarding culture, the transformative potential lies in cultivating a generative environment centered around a singular, compelling idea that resonates with everyone. In this book, "The Biology of Business," the aim is to simplify culture and infuse it with emotional resonance—not only to facilitate its shaping but also to accelerate its dissemination. Harnessing the power of simplicity and emotional connection ignites energy, fosters focus, and inspires decisive action within organizations. It also nurtures deeper engagement, resilience, and vested innovation among employees, driving long-term success.

The "frozen layer" as previously mentioned refers to a situation where individuals at the top of an organization want to improve, while those at the bottom desire growth and evolution. However, the middle layer—middle management—remains frozen and resistant to change. This layer requires rehabilitation, and it is crucial to gauge the pulse of employees who report to these managers. In a transparent ecosystem, it's essential to assess whether the manager can recover and redirect their efforts to align with the company's needs.

To illustrate the concept of the frozen layer, consider a software development company. The CEO aims to introduce new technologies to enhance the company's competitiveness, but middle management resists change. They are comfortable with existing technologies and do not perceive the need for a shift.

On the other hand managers who understand "people-first" and are in the right roles never people collect and are never driven by ego. They cultivate learning cultures by consistently engaging employees at the outset of each performance year: "What would you like to learn this year?"

The clarity of purpose, direction, and acknowledgment of individual employees are essential elements of a company's culture that must be in place for employees to thrive. An engaged, lean amplified learning system provides the perfect environment for employees to excel, enabling the company to impact the marketplace effectively.

When employees have time for learning in their work schedules, they see the value of their roles and the worthiness of their contributions. This facilitates the assimilation of new ideas, techniques, and technologies, which are critical for the organization's success.

In conclusion, a healthy and robust learning culture is vital to an organization's success. It serves as the heart and lungs of the company, providing the necessary oxygen and nutrients for every employee to perform optimally. Leadership plays a crucial role in fostering a purposeful and healthy culture. A successful company culture must be a learning culture where employees understand their roles, are accountable for their work, and are engaged in the company's success.

Transparency and appropriate information sharing are essential for creating a thriving company environment. The management structure should accurately interpret information from the CEO—often seen as the brain—without allowing ego to interfere. Moreover, the company's success hinges on employee motivation and engagement, which can be fostered through a genuinely functioning learning culture. Finally, tools like the Requisite Organization system and the Rapid Change Group curriculum are instrumental in achieving these goals.

CHAPTER FOUR

DISEASE

The impact of disease on the human body can be devastating, affecting both major and minor organs. Diseases can be classified into several categories, each serving a unique purpose in understanding how to contain, eradicate, or confront the inevitable. The four primary classes of disease are infectious diseases, deficiency diseases, hereditary diseases (which include both genetic and non-genetic hereditary conditions), and physiological diseases. While there are many diseases within each classification and additional categories beyond these, for the purposes of this discussion, we will focus on these four classes to avoid delving too deeply into epidemiology.

Disease represents the first of the five ways that businesses can fail, as it is a leading cause of human death worldwide. Infectious diseases are communicable and can be transmitted from one person to another through various means, such as respiratory droplets, bodily fluids, and other forms of contact. One example is the COVID variants, which are highly transmissible. In contrast, deficiency diseases are not infectious and are confined to the host or organism. Hereditary diseases, meanwhile, are passed down through genetic inheritance

In this case diseases are passed down from one family member to another, while physiological diseases are generally not communicable or spreadable. However, any illness that begins with a virus or bacteria and causes diarrhea or vomiting can indeed spread.

When it comes to the impact of disease on an organization, infectious diseases are perhaps the most detrimental, as they can create outbreaks that are difficult to control, correct, or eradicate without significant effort and cost. This situation parallels what occurs within an organization when information is not shared openly, leading to a lack of transparency and a culture of rumor and misinformation—consequences that can have severe repercussions. While infectious diseases are not the only type that can affect an organization, they are by far the most damaging.

Diseases can significantly impact the human body, affecting different organs in various ways. For instance, infectious diseases can lead to a wide range of symptoms, from mild to severe, and can even be fatal.

Deficiency diseases can cause malnutrition, leading to stunted growth, weakened immune systems, and other health issues. Hereditary diseases can result in genetic mutations that cause various health conditions and disorders, while physiological diseases can disrupt the body's normal functions, resulting in chronic health problems.

One major organ system affected by disease is the cardiovascular system, which includes the heart, blood vessels, and blood. Diseases that impact this system can cause a wide range of symptoms, including chest pain, shortness of breath, dizziness, and fainting. Cardiovascular diseases can also lead to heart attacks, strokes, and other serious health issues.

Another major organ affected by disease is the respiratory system, which includes the lungs, trachea, bronchi, and other structures. Diseases that impact this system can cause breathing difficulties, coughing, wheezing, and other symptoms. Respiratory diseases can also lead to chronic conditions such as asthma and chronic obstructive pulmonary disease (COPD).

The digestive system is similarly vulnerable, encompassing the liver, stomach, intestines, and other components. Diseases affecting this system can result in symptoms such as abdominal pain, bloating, diarrhea, and constipation. Digestive diseases can also lead to serious conditions like liver failure and cancer.

The nervous system, which includes the brain, spinal cord, and nerves, is also susceptible to disease. Disorders in this system can manifest as headaches, dizziness, seizures, and muscle weakness. Neurological diseases can lead to conditions such as Alzheimer's disease and Parkinson's disease.

Deficiency diseases, while not communicable, can still cause significant harm to both individuals and organizations. These diseases arise when the body lacks essential nutrients, such as vitamins, minerals, or proteins. In the context of an organization, deficiencies can manifest in various forms. For example, if an organization lacks necessary resources—such as financial capital, supply chain efficiency, or human capital— it can lead to deficiencies that impact overall performance, resulting in low quality or an inability to meet customer demand. Additionally, a lack of diversity or a variety of skill sets can hinder an organization's ability to adapt and innovate.

Hereditary diseases are those passed down genetically from one generation to another. In the context of an organization, this can refer to inherited cultural or behavioral patterns that may impact operations. For example, if an organization has a history of resisting change or adopting new technologies, this may be an inherited trait that is difficult to overcome. Inherited traits can also include issues such as nepotism, where family members or friends are favored for positions over more qualified candidates, and a lack of diversity in leadership roles.

Physiological diseases, while not communicable, can still have a significant impact on both individuals and organizations. These diseases affect the body's physical functioning and can hinder a person's ability to work effectively. In an organizational context, physiological diseases can refer to workplace injuries or chronic health issues that affect an employee's job performance. For example, an employee with chronic back pain may struggle to perform physically demanding tasks, impacting their productivity and overall contribution to the organization.

So, how can an organization protect itself from the impact of disease? Just as a healthy lifestyle can help prevent disease in individuals, a healthy organizational culture can mitigate the negative effects of disease within a company. This means fostering a culture of transparency, open communication, and diversity. By promoting open communication, an organization can prevent the spread of rumors and misinformation that can harm its reputation and operations. By prioritizing diversity, an organization can ensure a range of skill sets and perspectives, enhancing its resilience and adaptability.

Creating a diverse culture enables teams to adapt and innovate in response to diverse customer demands and opportunities.

Additionally, by prioritizing employee well-being and creating a safe work environment, an organization can mitigate the negative impact of physiological diseases on its workforce.

Diseases can also affect various parts of the body, including the skin, eyes, muscles, hair, and bones. Nothing is immune to the potential impact of disease, and the same is true for organizations. Lean thinking, which promotes a systems approach to work, suggests, "If you are going to change something in a system, you should examine the entire system." If one part of the system is altered, then everything may be subject to reevaluation. A system does not operate independently; it must be monitored, maintained, and transformed as needed. Google exemplifies this with its ongoing, comprehensive transformation. Did you know that Google has the capability to complete over one thousand software releases a day? That is efficient and incredibly lean.

Now, let's embark on a mental journey together. (By the way, there will be several more of these journeys ahead.) At times, you will need to play different roles and allow yourself to embody the traits and characteristics necessary to grasp the essence of each journey. In many of these scenarios, you'll need to be yourself, but not in your usual capacity. Think back to your earlier days—where you came from. If you started your own company and have always been the head honcho, then you will need to channel one of your employees. That's right: great CEOs know at least a handful of the lowest-paid employees in their companies. If you can see that these journeys might be difficult; adhere to the following advice to maximize the experience:

If you find yourself saying, "I do not know many of the lowest-paid employees in my company" (the janitorial staff, cafeteria staff, audiovisual team, those who restock coffee and water in your coolers, developers, line workers in the factories, supervisors, operators, or even the receptionist), then you must do the following:

Stop reading and arrange to have lunch with one of your employees.

Take the time to understand their world, their struggles, what they like about the company, and what could be improved. Share something personal from your own life to (1) humanize yourself to them—it will go a long way—and (2) briefly experience the vulnerability they face each day as they trust in and work for your company. (Please do this now if you need to. It's easy to pick this book back up and continue without missing a beat.)

If you haven't had this experience, the journeys will merely be a reading exercise and nothing more. If you believe that following my suggestion will offer you no benefit, then I encourage you to return the book to me, and I assure you your money will be refunded.

If you are ready and have had the aforementioned experience, then do the following:

Imagine you are one of your employees as you embark on these journeys. Do not approach them as a leader; what fun would that be? You'd get more of what you already have: your perspective. Ultimately, be anyone you want to be, just not the leader.

SCENARIO ONE

You work at a company with one hundred employees. One day, you arrive to find that your stuff has been moved to another space. You do a double take, keep walking, and then make a quick detour to your old office. Peering in, you see someone else's belongings carefully arranged on the walls and bookcase. The kicker is that you notice a new face sitting at your desk. While your new office isn't so bad, the whole move was done in secrecy. You say nothing because you actually like what you do and appreciate your new space, but you carry on as if nothing happened.

After settling into your new office, instead of calling your supervisor for answers, you check your email for any clues. You approach the early birds and overachievers in the office and ask, "Who is that?" (Truthfully, there's probably another part to that question: "and what the heck are they doing in my office?") Unfortunately, your supervisor is out for the next two days...

What do you think is going to happen?

SCENARIO TWO

You work for a company that has more than seventy-five thousand employees worldwide, making it the largest of its kind in your country. You attend a company-wide meeting, and the moderator announces, "Welcome to the blah, blah, blah all-staff meeting. I want to introduce the new CEO, Kathleen Applewood. Roger Snow, the former CEO, has decided to leave the company to pursue other opportunities, effective immediately."

Despite the moderator's attempts to present everything as okay or fine, your gut tells you otherwise. Several days later, you overhear one of Kathleen's direct reports say, "When the company fired Roger . . ."

At that moment, you realize the lack of transparency and its immediate impact on employees, including members of your own team. You didn't expect this. In fact, no one did. What do you think happens among managers in various roles, and how does that impact those further down the hierarchy? What do you think frontline employees will say to each other?

Regardless of how we want to perceive the situation, either scenario (which are real possibilities) will do little to foster purposeful inclusion, empathy, and trust. Whether you believe it or not, these qualities directly translate to the bottom line.

In the first scenario, rumors would start, and opinions would be shared about what happened. Within a week, everyone would know that something horrible had occurred. The truth is that, although the office change was made without employees' knowledge, it was a result of a lateral promotion Roger had requested nine months earlier. Here's the question you must answer to understand how these issues create deterioration: When the supervisor returned to the office, everything was already known, and he thought it would be a great surprise.

However, without transparency (like a note left on the desk that blew away), the truth rarely catches up with a rumor. For nearly a year, long after the situation was settled, this rumor continued to circulate, with some people never learning the real intent behind the move. What did the manager expect would happen? Was CMP involved here?

In the second scenario, trust was instantly eroded. It was noticeable in at least one virtual room as participants normally jovial with each other fell silent and literally said nothing the rest of the meeting. In a matter of hours, coworkers were sharing their opinions, and no one could believe the betrayal. Of course, for various reasons none of these professionals in this particular company would stay under that leadership. If there had been an attempt to be open and transparent in a consistent way, people would have been more forgiving with less information shared.

When trust is present, a leader can say I will share as much as I can with you, and then does, and people will trust them and continue to grant them permission to lead them.

Know that this is the nature of disease. It starts in a cloud of secrecy where in most cases the human organism does not realize or notice consciously that it is under attack. Often the realization comes from either a small discomfort or oddness noticed somewhere externally or internally, or overt pain. So how does this relate to your organization?

Initially, you most likely won't see the onset of a disease or its initial impact on your organization. However, you will begin seeing the long-term impact over time (if you are paying attention.) The unfortunate truth is that diseases are illnesses caused by harmful agents (pathogens) that get into your body.

The most common causes are viruses, bacteria, fungi, and parasites. At first glance at the causes, we'd tend to gravitate toward the parasites. We can easily apply the behavior of a parasite to that of our companies. In simple terms, they are a leech, eating away at the fabric of the organization. Unstopped and unchecked, all of the pathogens will kill off a system and eventually cause infection that can easily spread via multiple systems:

ORGANISM SYSTEMS AND ORGANIZATIONS

Integumentary	Policy that is learned coming through the door, expectations of new and all current employees and also campus buildings, feelings of safety, how people feel protected.
	Policies are not just for your company's protection (albeit mostly); they also serve as working agreements in many cases for all of your employees. This is the superficial part of the culture. (This system is the first layer of defense in keeping the organism healthy. It is the skin.)
Musculoskeletal	The system(s) people use to get their work done. These can be mental exercises or physical systems. (Ergonomic or not—why not the best for who really creates the money in the enterprise?) The systems carry the workload and move it toward completion. It is the part of the company that delivers customer satisfaction.
Urinary waste	Lean systems that keep the enterprise lean and healthy.
Respiratory the lungs	Training and learning system. (Recall from chapter three.)

Digestive	Remuneration system. (How people get Paid.) The digestive system extracts nutrients (excellence, quality, consistency from its employees), and there must be a reward back to the system so it can maintain itself. As well, see urinary above. (The bowels as part of the digestive system designed to absorb nutrients and expel waste.)
Endocrine	Formal meetings, water cooler moments, impromptu meetings. (This is where cells exchange hormones that either strengthen or weaken the enterprise.)
Lymphatic	Risk management and crisis response. (This is the response system to dangerous bacteria and viruses in the body.)
Reproductive	Succession planning, communities of practice that allow for knowledge transfers and like subsystem improvements.
Nervous	Not how we communicate, how what we communicate is translated and interpreted. (Does not work without a feedback loop for clarity.)
Circulatory	The heart, its pulse, its movement of the organism's lifeline, blood—also known as the culture. All systems impact each other. This one might be, however, the most powerful or at least the most needed for all of the systems.

We can now begin to imagine how these disease agents in the form of rumors, distrust, anger, discontentment, lack of transparency, leadership, shortcomings, apathy, and the like affect an organization. It is quite similar to the way we get exposed and or take bacteria, viruses, fungi, and parasites through various means into our bodies. There is an intruder alert moment, and the systems find ways to communicate and evaluate *together* the situation or disruption and then the response to issues, crises, escalations, options for defense, capabilities, etc. Then there is the response phase. This is when the body mounts a fight, every cell, organ, and system together, with everything they have.

Despite the availability of tools and tactics to overcome disease in an organization, many current practices inadvertently encourage dysfunction. For example, companies that are careless in their succession planning (discussed in Chapter 3) often allow managers to hire based on personal preferences, biases, and even unrecognized affinities in their screening processes. There is frequently no science, rhyme, or reason for how individuals enter a company structure, particularly in leadership teams.

As leaders, we tend to prioritize loyalty over future potential. This creates an environment where negative attitudes can quietly spread, as individuals—believing themselves to be valuable employees—propagate discontent instead of sharing knowledge or helping others improve. They may be performers who are disgruntled for various reasons but contribute little to the organization's betterment, balancing their praise with a consistent negative narrative. In many cases, personal affinities dictate hiring decisions, resulting in a "good ol' boy club" mentality. This does not mean that there are no women in the "good ol' boys club"; while there may not be enough representation, it indicates that a subculture of loyalty and trust will still emerge.

Ultimately this kind of culture implodes on itself over time, while keeping others from engaging in "deep" communications—even those who need to know. The outcome is disastrous. People become distrustful, float rumors, speak ill of the leadership, and, far worse, act insubordinately when they believe their behavior will go unnoticed.

With one of my consulting clients, I shared actual case studies under non-disclosure that described the type of company, its personnel, succession patterns, and current culture, based on interviews and pulse surveys. In almost every case, these organizations-including NGOs (Non-Governmental Organizations or non-profits)-struggled to fill their headcounts (no one wanted to work for them).

They suffered immense revenue losses (from training, retraining, recruiting, and high attrition), reduced budgets, made personnel cuts, restructured, and, by maintaining the good ol' boy network, ultimately failed. For them, it was too late.

For at least 90 percent of the other clients I have had the privilege of working with, they were able to "salvage" their operations. At the very least, they changed the way they communicated, fostering a more open environment that led to greater employee engagement and eventually saved their companies.

Here's another example of how disease can innocently creep into an organization: I was in a conversation with a group at a manufacturing company a year after COVID restrictions began to relax. It was a Saturday morning, and the company provided breakfast, pay, and some excellent speakers ahead of a public event on their campus. During the regular workweek, many employees were able to work remotely, while some were mandated to be in the office regularly, but intermittently (e.g., weekly, monthly, or multiple days in a week). One of the mandated employees expressed her opinion during one of the sessions, stating that being required to be in the office for three to five days was in direct conflict with the idea of flexible work. (Granted, she was there voluntarily on a Saturday morning.) Other employees were only required to come to the office once a month, but they had to navigate a laborious security checkpoint, which they complained about because it made entering the building cumbersome. To them, it felt as if they weren't a "normal" part of the company.

However, those mandated to be in the office daily dismissed the complaints about security, which instantly divided the conversation. After I had finished my presentation that morning, I was debriefing in a training room when a director-level person walked by and recognized someone else in the room with me. As we were being introduced, in walked the "divider." Now, to be fair, I do not believe this individual was malicious, mean, or lacking in empathy. In her defense, she had previously demonstrated a level of vulnerability and empathy not often seen in most companies. However, her comments, while emotionally motivated, were almost imperceptibly divisive. Not knowing the director, she made another comment about the necessity of being present in the office. Although she was simply expressing her feelings, she sparked another conversation as she left, which further highlighted the divide.

This division became even more apparent during a later seminar, where it quickly split the training room, creating a divide among participants with differing views. Unfortunately, this forum was not the appropriate setting for such a debate, leading to a disruption that was irreparable and allowing the matter to simmer unresolved without any attention paid to it or resolution for those it affected.

This unresolved yet top-of-mind topic would simmer across the company, one conversation after another. What a waste of time, money, and people hours. Left to its own course in the organization, it would foster a potential disease. It had already created a state of dis-ease.

Any kind of disease—whether physical, mental, infectious, non-infectious, deficiency, inherited, degenerative, social, or self-inflicted—can be deadly when left untreated, once it has struck an organism or an organization.

Before deciding to cut a single employee, understand that human organisms exhibit incredible resilience in the midst of chaos. In most cases, even the feeblest cell vows to fight. This is not to say that there won't be a need to make the usual cuts that companies believe they must implement to survive. However, recognize that each cell's survival instinct compels it to be part of the homeostatic process (remember homeostasis, the organism's desire to remain stable). Employees want things to be as expected and normal; they want to feel, "I can count on this organization to be there so that I can sustain myself and my family." This can often lead to a mindset of "I will do whatever it takes to help us succeed," which frequently includes the bad players who might have been responsible for either the onset of the disease or creating the opening for it to enter the organization.

At some later point, as is the case with a human organism, frequent checkups need to be conducted to ensure cells have not gone rogue.

By communicating appropriately, the cells know what they must do to keep the organization solvent and flourishing. Especially in cases of resurgence from near death, problem cells must be closely monitored and removed if, over time, they fail to maintain the fight or become ineffective. Having presented this alternative to further damaging the organization, it is important to note that when things are dire, sometimes the best solution is to rebuild trust, as mentioned earlier, and expose the source "on its way out the door."

There is, by the way, a connection between disease and dehydration. This fact has remained in my mind since I read a medical research journal article years ago highlighting its correlation to a worsening state of disease. In an organizational context, communication is the lifeblood of any organization. Without it, you and your organization will, in fact, die. (Two to three weeks without food before the worst begins, and only three to four days without water before all hell breaks loose.)

A coroner's plea:

Maintaining proper hydration is essential for our day-to-day bodily functions, such as regulating temperature, maintaining skin health, ensuring smooth muscle function, and promoting joint comfort. However, a recent study conducted by the National Institutes of Health (NIH) and published in the journal eBioMedicine has shown that drinking enough water is also associated with a significantly lower risk of developing chronic diseases, dying "early," or being biologically older than your chronological age.

The study's author, Natalia Dmitrieva, a researcher in the Laboratory of Cardiovascular Regenerative Medicine at the National Heart, Lung, and Blood Institute, stated that "the results suggest that proper hydration may slow down aging and prolong a disease-free life." The authors noted that learning preventive measures to slow the aging process is a major challenge in preventive medicine, especially as an epidemic of "age-dependent chronic diseases" emerges with the rapid aging of the world's population. Extending a healthy lifespan can significantly improve quality of life and decrease healthcare costs, more so than simply treating diseases.

To test their hypothesis, the researchers analyzed health data collected over thirty years from 11,255 participants of diverse ethnic backgrounds. They found that the biological age of these participants outpaced their chronological age by almost ten years. Those with high serum sodium levels, resulting from inadequate hydration, exhibited a 64 percent higher risk of faster aging and developing chronic diseases such as heart failure, stroke, atrial fibrillation, peripheral artery disease, chronic lung disease, diabetes, and dementia.

In conclusion, maintaining proper hydration is crucial not only for our day-to-day bodily functions but also, in terms of organizational communication, for a company's overall health and aging process.

By ensuring effective communication (staying properly hydrated), we may slow down the aging process within organizations and prolong a disease-free lifespan, ultimately improving quality of life and reducing remediation costs. In a very practical way, we can over hydrate our bodies. I would challenge the notion however, that we can over communicate in organizations.

Drink enough fluids every day: Communicate honestly, openly, and completely.

Once more, it's crucial to ask: Does your company culture genuinely reflect its purpose? Frequently, there's a significant gap between what a company claims its purpose is and what employees actually experience. By the way, any study referenced in this book may offer significant insights to support a single point, if that. My disclaimer is that all studies should invite scrutiny and challenge. However, the conclusion from various perspectives suggests that hydration, water, and communication (honest, open, and two-way) are critical to preventing premature aging.

In an organization, aging is synonymous with becoming antiquated, outdated, and eventually a dinosaur—a relic of the past. A lack of clear communication prevents the organization from being flexible enough to respond to external forces. Miscalculations in revenue streams (also known as value streams), changing market conditions (which are constantly evolving, whether you're attuned to them or not), attrition, poor succession planning, regulatory changes, and economic impacts are all reasons your organization must remain flexible.

Without proper hydration, your organization will become rigid and fail to function at peak levels.

CHAPTER FIVE

THE IMPACT OF AGING ON HUMAN ORGANISMS AND ORGANIZATIONS

Regardless of our willingness to acknowledge it, aging is an inevitable reality that affects various aspects of life, including the human organism, global infrastructures, organizational systems, hardware, and even thought processes. Everything we use or reference continuously experiences wear and tear due to friction, exposure, mechanical use, and the emergence of newer technologies or systems.

As a result, parts or systems may rust, erode, dissolve, wear thin, and ultimately crumble from repeated use and inherent weaknesses. For instance, in the human body, joints may require replacement due to degenerative disease, injury, or excessive use. Dehydration can also expedite the aging process, as discussed in previous chapters.

Similarly, organizations undergo aging processes that impact various components, including ideology, business systems, processes, and thinking patterns. These components, like the human organism, may function well initially but become unreliable over time due to outdated technology, logistics, security, ways of working, business systems, skills, and even ideas. The antidote is simple: aging often leaves clues that are particularly evident in the human organism. Thus, businesses are comparable to human organisms, sharing similar aging patterns and implications. To accommodate internal and external changes, organizations need to continually refresh and update their systems.

As we progress through life, our bodies inevitably undergo various changes that can affect our physical capabilities and overall well-being. These changes may include a loss of peak muscular abilities, a slowing metabolism, and a decline in overall system performance. As a result, our joints may become less resilient, and our muscles may experience more frequent pulls and pops. Our strength and reflexes may also diminish over time.

It's important to acknowledge that while many of us may be reluctant to admit it, these changes are a natural part of the aging process.

However, it's crucial to recognize that unless we actively work to maintain our physical, mental, and psychological abilities, we may lose them more rapidly than we would otherwise. This means taking steps to promote brain plasticity—the brain's ability to adapt and change—in order to mitigate the effects of aging.

When it comes to aging, it's not just individual human beings that are affected. Organizations can also experience age-related declines, just as our bodies and minds do. In this chapter, we will delve into the topic of senescence, or the process of aging. We will explore how cells age and die in the body and how this process can be compared to the aging and decline of organizational systems.

Additionally, we will examine the various impacts of aging on both human organisms and organizations and explore strategies for mitigating these effects. Finally, we will discuss the importance of innovation and adaptation in both individuals and organizations, as these qualities can help prolong health and success over time. Ultimately, the goal for biologists and organizational researchers is to better understand the aging process and to find ways to promote healthy aging in both people and organizations alike.

As we age, our bodies and minds undergo numerous changes that result in a decline in physical and cognitive abilities. At the cellular level, the aging process begins, and as cells age, they become less efficient and more prone to damage. This phenomenon is known as cellular senescence, which is one of the main causes of age-related diseases such as cancer, Alzheimer's disease, and osteoporosis.

Cellular senescence is triggered by various factors, including the shortening of telomeres, DNA damage, oxidative stress, and inflammation. Telomeres are the protective caps at the ends of chromosomes that shorten with each cell division. Once they become too short, the cell can no longer divide and enters a state of senescence.

While cellular senescence can help prevent the development of cancer by stopping damaged cells from dividing, the accumulation of senescent cells can also contribute to age-related diseases and a decline in overall health. As we age, it is important to take steps to mitigate the effects of cellular senescence, such as reducing oxidative stress and inflammation, paying particular attention to our intake of essential nutrients and supplements, and promoting healthy cell function.

Drawing a parallel between the aging process of the human body and organizational systems reveals that both have a limited lifespan and undergo decline over time. However, unlike cells, organizations have the potential to respawn and continue beyond their current usefulness; they can easily innovate and adapt to changes in their environment. Organizations that fail to do so—much like cells that cannot adapt—become less efficient and more prone to damage over time, ultimately leading to their decline and obsolescence.

A lack of innovation and adaptation is a primary cause of organizational decline. Organizations must adapt to changing market demands, consumer needs, and technological advancements to stay competitive. Similarly, a lack of investment in human capital can also contribute to organizational decline, as the health and success of an organization rely heavily on the skills, abilities, and productivity of its employees. By investing in employee development, organizations can foster a culture of innovation and creativity that helps mitigate the impacts of aging and decline.

Just as the human body must adapt to changes to maintain its health and vitality, organizations must also adapt to changes in their environment to remain relevant, successful, and competitive. Innovation, creating flexibility in systems to respond to challenges, and taking care of an organization's people are critical strategies for mitigating the effects of aging and decline in organizational systems.

Sometimes, however, the impacts of aging on human organisms and organizations can be significant. In humans, aging can lead to a decline in physical and cognitive abilities, an increased risk of disease and injury, and a decrease in overall quality of life. In organizations, aging can result in declines in productivity, quality, customer satisfaction, and profitability. Aging in humans can weaken immune system function, making individuals more vulnerable to infections and diseases, as well as impair cognitive abilities, including memory, attention, and processing speed, which can make learning new skills and adapting to changes in the environment more challenging.

In organizations, aging can lead to decreased productivity due to a lack of innovation and a decline in work quality. Seasoned employees may become resistant to change and less adaptable to new technologies and processes, ultimately affecting the organization's competitiveness and profitability.

However, there are strategies that can be employed to mitigate the impacts of aging on both humans and organizations. Regular exercise, a healthy diet, and stress reduction techniques can help maintain physical and cognitive health in humans. Staying socially engaged and intellectually stimulated can also keep the mind sharp and prevent cognitive decline. Medical interventions, such as hormone replacement therapy, can be effective in managing age-related symptoms.

In organizations, the most prominent way to combat the aging process is to invest in people. This can be achieved through training and development programs that help maintain a skilled and adaptable workforce.

Encouraging innovation and experimentation can help keep the organization competitive and adaptable to changes in the marketplace.

Overall, while aging is an inevitable process, there are strategies that can be employed to lessen its impacts on both humans and organizations. By focusing on maintaining physical and cognitive health in humans, as well as investing in human capital and innovation in organizations, we can prolong health and success. (Human capital includes assets like education, training, intelligence, skills, health, and other attributes employers value, such as loyalty and punctuality.)

In addition to these strategies, innovation and adaptation are critical for both human organisms and organizations to maintain health and corporate prosperity. For humans, the ability to adapt to environmental changes is essential for survival. This includes adjustments to diet, climate, and social structures. The capacity to innovate and create new technologies and tools has also allowed humans to thrive and dominate the planet.

Similarly, organizations that fail to innovate and adapt will eventually decline and become obsolete. Innovation enables organizations to develop new products and services, improve efficiency, and remain competitive as the market evolves. Change is a constant, as we often hear; you be the judge.

While "everything changes" may not be a scientific principle in itself, it is a concept supported by many scientific theories. In physics, for example, the concept of entropy states that the universe is always moving toward disorder and randomness means that everything is constantly changing. In biology, the theory of evolution tells us that living organisms are always adapting over time. Similarly, in psychology, the concept of neuroplasticity explains how the brain can change and adapt throughout an individual's lifetime. While "everything changes" may not be a specific scientific principle, it is a fundamental concept supported by various scientific theories. Adaptation allows organizations to respond to market changes, such as shifts in consumer preferences or new technologies.

As mentioned earlier, the success of Google can be attributed to its culture of innovation, which enables it to adapt and overcome challenges. Other successful companies, like Primo Water, OOFOS, Apple, and Amazon, also prioritize innovation and continuous improvement to stay ahead in the market by providing exceptional value to their customers.

Inevitably, everything will age—whether it's you, me, our thinking, cultures, ways of working, workforce habits, skills, or technology. This aging process will lead to a measurable decline in both living organisms and organizations, potentially impacting physical and cognitive abilities and affecting overall quality of life.

However, with the right strategies, the impacts of aging can be greatly mitigated. Exercise is perhaps the most effective strategy for helping individuals maintain a necessary level of fitness and improve overall health.

The human body is designed to be active often, if not daily; it is not built for a sedentary lifestyle. Similarly, business organizations are not meant to be static. As living, dynamic entities, organizations create an energy that must be continually maintained to remain alive and healthy.

Keeping organizations healthy and responsive to aging is essential. A nutritious diet can provide the human body with the necessary fuel to function optimally. Stress-reduction techniques, such as mindfulness and meditation, can help individuals manage stress and improve mental health, enabling them to perform at their peak—much like we desire our cells to function.

Investing in people is perhaps the most effective way to mitigate the impacts of aging. Helping employees learn new skills, acquire knowledge, and stay updated with the latest developments in their fields can help them remain competitive and relevant, reflecting the company's intent. For organizations, investing in employee development programs is crucial for enhancing skills, capabilities, and engagement. When executed well, these programs keep the spirit of innovation alive by fostering a sense of reinvention alongside the company, resulting in increased productivity, innovation, and profitability.

If you're wondering why investing in employee development consistently yields results, it's because humans are inherently designed to think and grow. Many people would choose to continue working into their seventies when given the chance and flexibility, especially when they feel valued. There was a time when the term "semi-retired" described individuals who worked not out of financial necessity but for the joy of contributing.

The benefits of investing in your people are clear: with age comes wisdom, particularly in decision-making. Additionally, the ability to think long-term improves. This is evident in the leadership styles of many successful CEOs.

Dr. Jacques's work focused on a population ranging from age twenty-one to eighty. His research clearly indicates that the complexity of mental processing tends to grow with age within any organization. This suggests that making numerical headcount reductions based solely on salaries and strict metrics could be a mistake. Instead, decisions should be guided by the question of whether a person is providing value—assessed through circular feedback loops involving those they interact with, including supervisors and immediate colleagues. (Of course, this should not be perceived as a witch hunt; there are strategic ways to gather this information respectfully.)

Interestingly, in many countries, the executive suite traditionally includes leaders who are eighty years or older. The ideal scenario lies in creating a cultural mix that encourages innovation from newer generations while honoring and inviting the traditions of seasoned workers. This fosters a deeper understanding of company history, ultimately leading to greater innovation. Additionally, rather than viewing seasoned workers solely as financial investments, challenge them with the latest products and associated challenges—they will often surprise you. They typically have a vested interest in safeguarding the company's interests to a higher degree than newer employees, whose tenure may be uncertain.

When executed correctly, the fusion of their ideas with those of newer thinkers consistently yields superior solutions compared to either group acting alone. A pertinent example illustrates this point: in the mid-2000s, a sizable chemical company faced a near-catastrophic incident due to a hierarchical flaw in its operations.

Over a holiday weekend, a tank containing caustic materials began leaking. Despite having both a new hire and seasoned employees on standby, the absence of a crucial seasoned (CMP) management-level employee in the contingency plan resulted in a failure to contain the situation effectively. Over 18,000 people were evacuated from their homes on a late Sunday evening because of the leak.

This incident underscored the necessity of having the right individuals in key positions to prevent business catastrophes. Innovation, collaboration, and trust between new hires and seasoned employees are pivotal in addressing challenges, yet these elements were absent from the culture. The failure to acknowledge this critical structural requirement proved not only financially detrimental but also irreparably damaging to the company's reputation within the community, highlighting the importance of vested individuals in protecting and advancing the company's interests.

Employee development programs, regardless of biological age, enhance the skills necessary for adaptation, as skill development itself is a form of adaptation. The ability to expand one's value to their craft, the organization, or simply the love for what they do will always be rooted in an employee's value system, as previously mentioned.

Employee engagement is critical; when employees are not engaged, you end up with a workforce that merely punches a time clock, does the minimum, complains, and fosters a negative culture that ultimately erodes the very fabric of your organization.

On the other hand, drawing from brain plasticity, a robust culture of innovation can only emerge from a focused effort on fostering it. When there is no focus on innovation, it becomes a daydream—a fleeting thought. By providing opportunities for employees to learn and grow, organizations can enhance the overall knowledge base and expertise of their workforce, leading to increased productivity, better decision-making, and more effective problem-solving. Isn't this why we exist as business organizations? We exist to solve problems for our customers. They want something they do not have, and we can provide it.

Furthermore, by promoting a culture of continuous learning and improvement, organizations can foster a genuine sense of innovation and creativity among employees, resulting in new ideas, products, and services that drive profitability and growth.

However, it's worth noting that the effectiveness of employee development programs can depend on various factors, such as the quality of the training and resources provided, the relevance of the training to employees' roles and responsibilities, and the extent to which the organization supports and encourages ongoing learning and development.

Learning is never just training. Training is never merely a certification. And certification does not guarantee competence. Learning is truly magical, and that is not to undervalue it in any way. As one of my mentors once taught me, you are taking a space within a living organism and literally inserting something into it. Once the information is within the organism, it can choose to act upon that information and, under the right circumstances, use it to perform basic or remarkable human behaviors—namely, to adapt, overcome, and survive. This is behavior modification at its finest: teaching people to change.

This is what Einstein meant when he suggested that a rubber band stretched would never return to its original form. This is what it means to live: adjusting to an ever-changing world around us and interacting with it without the stress of surviving based on what we have learned.

Because the world is constantly evolving, those who can adapt to change are the ones who will thrive. Therefore, it is essential for individuals and organizations to embrace a culture of learning and continuous improvement. This can involve seeking out new experiences, learning from mistakes, and being open to feedback and new ideas. At one particular company I worked with, employee teams are encouraged to hold "screw-up parties." These gatherings take place after iterative work is completed, where teams celebrate and laugh about failed innovative efforts and the lessons learned from their mistakes.

As one of the greatest business minds I know often suggests, if you can master this principle alone, you will have created an innovative culture in reverse. This is one of the "secret sauces" of successful businesses. Why? Because we know for certain that Thomas Edison did not create the incandescent light bulb on his very first attempt. It was only after numerous failed attempts and discussions with his colleagues about those failures that he was able to perfect it.

By implementing these practices, individuals and organizations can remain competitive, stay ahead of the curve, and achieve long-term success, despite the inevitability of aging and change.

While aging is a natural process that cannot be avoided, its impacts can be eased through various strategies, such as "moving", eating better, minimizing your stressors, as well as investing in the advancement of people, the human capital within organizations.

However, in order to maintain a healthy system, organizations must also embrace a culture of innovation and adaptation and continuously strive to improve themselves and their processes. By doing so, they can overcome the challenges of an ever-changing, aging world and move closer to their goals.

CHAPTER SIX

A CONVERSATION BETWEEN A CORONER AND AN ORGANIZATIONAL HEALTH CONSULTANT

The concept of organizational death is often overlooked in business management. Many companies fail to recognize the signs of impending demise and continue to operate inefficiently until it is too late. We will begin our final descent to a safe landing in this book by sharing a conversation between a coroner and a consultant discussing the similarities between human organisms and business organizations, particularly how they die.

This conversation will highlight the various signs and symptoms of organizational death, as well as the steps that can be taken to prevent it.

The coroner will draw on her understanding of the signs and symptoms of death in human organisms. She will explain how the body shuts down, how vital signs change, and how the brain ceases to function, becoming a "neglecta sine gratia"—a person who is ignored, unappreciated, and irrelevant. She will then compare these symptoms to the signals that precede organizational death.

The coroner will discuss how companies often experience a decline in profits, a decrease in customer satisfaction, and a drop in employee morale. She will emphasize that, just as with human organisms, it is crucial to recognize these signs early and take action to prevent further decline.

The consultant will then share his perspective on the topic, beginning with the importance of creating a healthy organizational culture. He will stress that, much like human organisms, a healthy culture is essential for the long-term survival of the organization. The consultant will discuss several simple steps that can be taken to foster a healthy culture, such as promoting complete and transparent communication, encouraging collaboration, providing opportunities for growth and development, and nurturing genuine connections to build a thriving community within the organization.

The conversation will then shift to the steps that can be taken to prevent organizational death. The coroner will reiterate that, just as with human organisms, prevention is key. She will discuss the importance of monitoring vital signs—such as customer satisfaction and employee morale—and taking action to address any issues that arise. The consultant will then offer his insights on steps that can be taken to avert organizational death, including implementing a continuous improvement process, staying up-to-date with industry trends, and investing in employee training and development early on and taking action to prevent further decline.

The coroner will emphasize that, just as with human organisms, it is possible to extend the life of a business organization by taking proactive steps to promote a healthy culture and prevent decline. The consultant will then offer some final words of wisdom, such as the importance of embracing change, staying nimble, and remaining open to new ideas and perspectives, rather than adopting the ego-driven mindset of "we've always done it this way, and we will continue to do it this way."

The conversation between the coroner and the consultant highlights the similarities between human organisms and business organizations in decline. By recognizing the signs of deterioration and taking initiative-taking steps to foster a healthy organizational culture, it is possible to extend the life of a business and prevent premature death. The dialogue emphasizes the importance of staying vigilant, understanding the implications of warning signs, and taking action to address emerging issues as they arise. By following these steps, companies can cultivate a culture of constant and never-ending improvement to ensure long-term success.

Here is the conversation:

The consultant walked into the coroner's office and found her sitting at her desk, surrounded by stacks of papers and files. The coroner looked up and smiled at the consultant.

"Ah, good to see you," she said. "I've been looking forward to this conversation today."

The consultant smiled back and took a seat. "I was hoping to pick your brain about something," he said. Given that the coroner had run a major office for twenty-six years, serving eighteen million people, the consultant believed she might have valuable insights based on her experience with large organizations, budgets, personnel changes, economic responses, technological shifts, and common issues faced by businesses.

The coroner leaned back in her chair and steepled her fingers. "I see," she said. "Well, I've seen plenty of organizations die in my time, that's for sure. What specifically are you interested in?"

"I've been thinking about how the process of an organization dying is similar to that of a human body," the consultant replied. "There are stages of decay, just like there are stages of growth, aging, and even illness."

The coroner nodded. "I can see where you're coming from," she said. "There are certainly similarities. But let's dive a little deeper. What specific stages of decay are you referring to?"

"Well," the consultant said, "I think there's denial, where the organization refuses to acknowledge that anything is wrong. Then there's anger, where people start blaming each other for the problems. Next is bargaining, where they try to make deals to fix the issues. After that comes depression, where they start to lose hope. And finally, there's acceptance, where they realize the organization is dying and people need to start planning for the future."

The coroner listened thoughtfully. "That is incredibly insightful, and I see how easily you connected business behavior to some human psychological stages. "You've really thought about this," she said. "I have, through nearly 4 decades of work experience," the consultant quickly responded.

"But I would argue that there are a few more stages," the coroner continued. "For example, there's the stage of disintegration, where the organization starts to break apart. Then there's the stage of dissolution, where it finally disappears altogether."

"That's a good point," the consultant said. "I can see how those stages would fit in. But what causes an organization to go through these stages in the first place? Is it the same as what happens in organisms biologically?"

The coroner leaned forward, her eyes gleaming. "That's the million-dollar question," she said. "There are many factors that can contribute to the death of an organization. In many cases, they are the same as those affecting an organism—if you understand the comparison. Sometimes it's external factors, like changes in the market or new technology that renders the organization obsolete. Other times, it's internal factors, like poor management or a toxic culture. Often, that is where the million dollars is spent—fixing a toxic culture and addressing other internal issues. People like you, who have the answers, are the fixers."

"I've seen that happen," the consultant said. "But what do you think an organization can do to prevent these issues? Is there anything they can do to avoid the stages of decay, in your opinion?"

The coroner leaned back in her chair again and tapped her chin. "That's a tough one," she said. "There's no foolproof way to prevent an organization from dying. However, there are things that can help. For example, having a strong culture that values innovation—where employees actively seek out new ideas as a means of survival and adapt to changes—can significantly enhance a company's ability to thrive. This is quite similar to the human body.

Additionally, having good leadership that is willing to make tough decisions can also make a difference. Sometimes a leading product line may have outlived its usefulness or is losing revenue and market share compared to newer, faster, and better services or products.

The consultant nodded. "Those are good points," he said. "But I think there's always a role for good consultants like me. We help organizations identify weaknesses in their structures and processes, as well as areas that can be improved. We then work with them to develop strategies to address those issues."

The coroner smiled. "Absolutely," she said. "I think consultants can be unbelievably valuable in that way. Good consultants are like effective alternative medicine; they often work better than conventional preventive measures. Maybe more on that later. As I mentioned, leadership needs to be the most flexible and adaptable person in the entire organization. Any leader without flexibility is bound for major issues. Adhering to a regimen of stretching or being guided by someone who knows how to adapt can be invaluable. Unfortunately, there are not enough great consultants in the world to help all leaders become these flexible individuals."

"What do you mean by that?" asked the consultant.

"The number of businesses active and inactive across the world is innumerable. The attempts to grow a thriving throughout history will almost outnumber the world's population multiple times, as each person can start and fail at many businesses in their lifetime. Simply put, not every business will succeed. Those that do have two hidden characteristics. The first is that the leaders of these companies never lose sight of the fact that wisdom and good counsel are as important as knowing how to read, manipulate, and execute strategies for their organization to achieve the bottom line."

She continued, "The second characteristic is that they understand the human element of empathy and can almost naturally assimilate how they feel internally and be proprioceptively aware of their organization. This works two ways: first, they can empathize with their employees on a workload level; second, they sincerely experience what employees feel on an acute emotional level. They know when to push for innovation and when employees are ready to embrace change because that change has been communicated effectively."

The consultant interrupted, asking, "I think I know what proprioceptive means from a past career. In what context do you mean it?"

The coroner responded, "It refers to movement and how an organism perceives itself moving in relation to itself—simple 360-degree awareness! It's like the human brain; it knows where it is and where all its parts are in space at any given time."

Finally, the consultant said, "If I owned my own company, what would you tell me is the most important thing to consider, How would you help me run my company in the best way possible—specifically, to avoid major preventable issues?"

Her final pieces of advice were phenomenal. She stood up and slowly paced behind her large desk before saying, "Always maintain your integrity, which is linked to humility. That will guide your company's ethics. Remember that how you go, so goes your company." Body parts know what is going on with any part of the body that is suffering, exhibiting inefficiencies, pain, or degeneration. Your employees can figure you out just as quickly as a sneeze occurs. If you have an ego, your managers will, too—and you're doomed. If you have a laissez-faire attitude, this will trickle down to your employees, and they will treat your business the same way you do. If you show them empathy, they will show your business empathy and work harder because they care and trust you.

"Remember that perception rules until the truth is revealed, and even then it can be difficult to convince some." Monitor your perception so you can instantly separate it from potential facts. Data is king, but only if it has been vetted by an independent source willing to be brutally honest. This also means you must always be willing to accept the truth.

"Next, always be willing to listen to your employees." They are the rubber on your company's wheels. You may see the pothole they are about to hit as the driver, but they will, in fact, be the ones experiencing it. Make the ride as comfortable for them as possible, and they will reward you and the company in turn.

"Find a consultant to talk to before big decisions are made." A really good consultant should have some business experience, but they do not have to be 'you' to help you excel at being you.

A good coach or consultant should have a high CMP. They should possess skills and knowledge about your industry and value people more than they value their programs, money, ego, or results. This means empathy, and you should ask them the following question within the first hour of conversation—perhaps even as your first question: "What do you think about empathy?" If their answer, no matter how it is paraphrased, is anything other than, "It is the most important thing to have when working with people," "run— and I mean run—fast. It doesn't matter whether they are from the Big Four or an independent consultant; the latter may be preferable because many of the good ones don't work for larger firms. They are thinkers, not robotic system implementers. The person you need should understand the value of the bottom line and know that, in any business organization, people come first.

This is not just an 'agile way of working,' a good business principle, or a new fad—it is the only way to work. Every implemented system should start with people, and every good consultant and coach knows this.

"Lastly, a consultant may bring you a program. If you cannot understand it, choose not to use it." If your employees need something specific and your consultant cannot create it, find another one quickly. When you do implement any change, take a moment to check in with your employees. Call them, invite them to your office, and ask what value they are getting from it and what they would change. Find out how they feel about it."

"Remember, if employees have a collective dislike for a new implementation, it may indicate a misalignment within the company's structure." This could involve finance, engineering, operations teams, architects, service providers, communications teams, or even simple policies that prevent employees from feeling comfortable. If this happens, your change or implementation will face resistance. People will only make uncomfortable changes if they can fully see the benefits.

"Ultimately, it's the organization's responsibility to take action and implement the necessary changes to ensure its survival, and that begins with you."

"Without proper attention, organizations can become sick and diseased, leading to their eventual death. It's important for leaders to monitor the health of their organization just as they would their own bodies."

The consultant responded, "Wow, how insightful! I completely agree. Just like the human body, there are warning signs that an organization may be in trouble. For example, high turnover rates or a lack of innovation could indicate a deeper problem."

"Yes," said the coroner, "and often these warning signs are ignored or dismissed until it's too late. Leaders must be proactive in addressing these issues and seeking help when needed. Just as a person may seek medical attention when they're not feeling well, organizations should consult experts in their field when they're struggling."

"That's a great point," replied the consultant. "Just as different illnesses require different treatments, various organizational problems necessitate tailored solutions. It's crucial to identify the root cause of an issue and customize the solution accordingly."

"Exactly," said the coroner. "It's not just about finding a solution; it's about implementing it effectively. Just as a person may need to change their lifestyle or take medication to treat an illness, an organization might need to make significant changes to its structure or culture to address the problem."

"Right, and while those changes may be difficult or uncomfortable at first, they're necessary for the long-term health of the organization. It's important to keep the end goal in mind and remain committed to the process, remembering that people are the key to all change—not just the idea or program," the consultant replied.

"In the same way a person needs to make ongoing efforts to maintain their health, organizations must constantly monitor and adjust their practices to ensure they remain healthy and fit. It's a continuous process that requires attention and effort," said the coroner.

The consultant added, "That's very true. Just as a person's health can affect their entire life, the health of an organization can impact its employees, customers, and the community as a whole. It's essential for leaders to recognize the broader implications of their decisions and prioritize the health of their organization accordingly."

"Indeed," the coroner chimed in. "In the end, organizations are made up of people, and their health and well-being should always be the top priority. Just as a person's health affects every aspect of their life, the health of an organization impacts every facet of its operations. By taking care of the organization's health, leaders are ultimately caring for the people within it. It's a win-win solution that benefits everyone involved."

The consultant then stood up, saying, "Well said. I've used the entire time you allotted me. It's clear that there are many similarities between the health of the human body and that of an organization. By recognizing and addressing warning signs, tailoring solutions, implementing them effectively, and making ongoing efforts to maintain health, leaders can ensure the long-term success of their organizations."

"I couldn't agree more. It's a challenging but rewarding process, and one that's absolutely essential for the survival and growth of any organization," retorted the coroner. "Thank you for this conversation. It's been enlightening to see the parallels between my work and the world of business."

"Likewise," he replied. "I think we can all learn something from the way you approach your work and apply those lessons to our own organizations. Thanks for sharing your insights. This has been a really interesting conversation."

"My pleasure. It's always great to have these kinds of discussions and exchange ideas with someone who has a keen yet unrestricted perspective on growth, intent, and value."

Take care, and good luck with your ongoing work to help businesses function at their highest and best levels."

"You too," said the consultant, as they shook hands, "Enjoy the rest of your day."

CHAPTER SEVEN

CONCEPTS TO EXECUTION (WHAT WE'VE GAINED FROM OUR LEARNING JOURNEY)

We've been on a journey—a journey that has taken us through human anatomy at a high yet relevant level. We have explored business through the lens of our anatomy and how it functions as a cohesive system. In this section, we will reflect on the insights from each chapter, highlighting key points to consider and utilize when appropriate.

As we prepare to land our flight and conclude our journey, I want to share a thought about a perspective many of us possess but few recognize it as a call to action. The world of work is changing, and it has already transformed significantly. This evolution continues, coinciding with an economic downturn (the Benner Cycle) and shifting customer demands and then bull markets. In small ways, we are all aware of these changes.

I refer to this as the "tornado perspective." When we find ourselves in the midst of the tornado, with everything spinning around us—including ourselves—we often struggle to see what is truly swirling inside that whirlwind unless it is right in front of us.

We may catch glimpses of some things, but not enough to fully understand or leverage them to our advantage. Conversely, anyone who comprehends what they are observing in you or your organization can not only see you and the chaos surrounding you but may also offer perspectives on your risks and how to avoid harm or damage to your organization when the spinning slows and things begin to settle.

How you respond to the changes that most organizations lack a change management plan for—the post-pandemic economic era, which is akin to a five to ten year plan, political and policy instability, diversity advantages, workforce expectations and challenges —will determine your business's fate. I am not alone in this perspective; other thought leaders share similar insights. The question is: will you be an early adopter, emerging from this era with incredible margins and have a satisfied workforce, or will you struggle because you chose to ignore the warnings?

Dave Ramsey, a favorite financial podcaster for many, often provides valuable insights as a thought leader because he fundamentally understands the human element of business leadership.

In a recent interview with "The Street," he expressed a sentiment that resonates with this discussion, speaking about employees in the post-pandemic era: "Employees today are demonstrating a newly developing work ethic. The exceptional ones are unafraid of hard work. They're passionate, intelligent, and mission driven. They'll charge the gates of hell with water pistols for something they believe in."

But that means you have to provide meaning in the work they do. Employees want to see that their efforts connect to something that matters. They seek to be treated with dignity, not merely as units of production or numbers. Most of them have inquiring minds and want to understand why you do things the way you do.

Ramsey also offers a word of caution on how to engage the evolving workforce:

> "These new types of employees can be the worst two generations to work for someone who's just a boss. That's because bosses push while leaders pull. If you're going to pull, you must inform, communicate, and share a vision that draws people into your mission. Bosses, for the most part, adopt a 'do it this way because I said so' attitude. That approach won't last long with Gen Z-ers and millennials."
>
> They are, for the most part, genuine, real people and hard workers. If you provide what they need as a leader, they'll astonish you with their intelligence and what they're capable of achieving!

While I'm not the only one ringing the alarm about how we engage our workforces in this current age, it's becoming increasingly clear through interviews with thought leaders that our workforce is changing. This shift is neither inherently good nor bad; it ultimately depends on your perspective (more on that in the next section).

The "Thought Leadership" section addresses how you, as a leader or group of leaders, should engage with all levels of your organization—not just the "trusted few." Transparency will always convey authenticity. Learning to communicate at deeper levels consistently yields positive results. As my colleague, brain scientist Horacio Sanchez from Resiliency Inc., once said, "Communication is your friend, and language can often be your enemy."

This theme will also be explored in the "Thought Leaders" section. Be aware that change is inevitable; if you get ahead of the curve, your organization can not only survive but thrive. Understanding your organization's dynamics as intimately as you understand your own body—an intention of this book—will help you view challenges as pebbles rather than potholes.

Reflecting on our examination of failed businesses, it's essential to recall the reasons behind their demise. They often lacked innovation, adaptability, and effective leadership. Failures were typically rooted in critical dysfunctions within the organization—be it in its major components or essential functions.

We discovered that innovation thrives in environments where employees trust the system, feel empowered to lead, and possess the necessary skills. The implications point to the importance of developing a culture that supports these principles.

A learning culture is essential for sustaining an enterprise, much like the vitamins and nutrients required for a healthy human organism.

When companies fail to promote learning across the organization, growth becomes stunted, leading to a loss of functionality and an inability to support the whole.

This marks the beginning of their decline. The same is true for the human organism; poor anatomy in any organization contributes to less valuable products and can ultimately lead to reductions in force or even non-existence. This applies to any product or industry.

I once served as an administrator for a service offered in the Southeastern USA. After assembling a strong team, we set out to market, sell, and sustain our services across a specific region of the state. Each department—each critical organ of the organization—was firing on all cylinders, and we were making progress. However, well into our six-county region, things began to sputter. Our marketing had lost its edge, and customer interest begin to decline. In hindsight, we concluded—several years after going out of business—that the marketing director had other interests that adversely affected both the output of the team and the department's commitment to understanding our customers' needs.

With this lost growth came a diminishing pipeline of customers.

It wasn't just marketing, though; the dysfunction in that department impacted sales, which in turn affected finances. If we had fostered a learning culture, the employees in that department could have better navigated the departure—both mentally and physically—of their leadership until a capable successor was found.

We also examined how organs function both separately and in conjunction with one another, as no organ—just like any part of an organization—can operate in isolation. Over time, as we adjust our perspectives, we begin to see that organizations function much like living organisms, particularly humans. This underscores the importance of continuously nurturing the systems within the organism or organization. When the well-being of "the people"—the cells that do the work—takes top priority, they tend to perform effectively.

The failure of any system or organ can significantly impact the entire organism, forcing other organs to compensate for the reduced value of the failing component. This principle applies to customer value as well.

In a business organization, any part that fails to produce results at a high level can lead to serious negative outcomes. These repercussions can create a slippery slope toward nonexistence, putting the entire organization at risk.

As a leader, you bear the responsibility of monitoring the vital signs of your organization. You need to know the pulse, the blood pressure—how hard people are working—and how effectively information is disseminated. These aspects must be prioritized. However, remember to look beyond the numbers. Confirm their accuracy by discussing what they mean with your people and inviting their feedback. How else will you know if each part is functioning optimally?

One effective approach we discussed for keeping a business operating well is to ensure we are nourishing the organization as we would a living organism. The system must be fed with the best resources available.

Nutrients are essential for the system to function as a complete, smooth, and synchronized entity. When challenges arise, if the structure and management have not provided the appropriate nutrients, it can ultimately harm the body—and any business as well.

The nutrients consumed and utilized by the system create the culture within an organization. How this system functions and perceives itself constitutes the framework of its culture. A company's culture is like a living, flowing, shapeable, and pulsating set of values, traditions, and ways of working. This culture shapes the habits of its employees, and if left unattended, it may be influenced by the most vocal and dominant personalities or arbitrary selectors, potentially leading to poor leadership and a dysfunctional work environment. Culture must never be left to develop on its own; it should be nurtured, shaped, and maintained. A company's culture is like water, following the path of least resistance and flowing to its lowest point. In contrast, a purposeful and intentional culture is cultivated through focused effort and a clear vision, which involves regular discussions, gathering real data, and addressing issues.

Culture and its success within any company depend on the transparency of information shared across the organization and how employees understand and execute it. The timelier and more relevant the information, the more likely employees are to engage with the company's vision, values, goals, and processes.

In developing culture—however you envision it—employees must recognize that learning is key, normal, and necessary for their growth as a working group.

This is to say that people come to expect, participate in, and screen their results through what they define as a learning culture.

Once the philosophy of a learning culture has been adopted, it becomes easier to integrate clarity of purpose, direction, and acknowledgment of individual employees into a company's culture. In this scenario, even those who are slightly engaged can benefit and thrive.

An engaged, lean, amplified learning system creates the ideal environment for employees to excel.

Ultimately, the company's success hinges on employees' motivation and engagement, which can be fostered through a truly functioning learning culture.

Like any living system, adaptations and adjustments are necessary— especially in the face of challenges, shifts, and even disease. Despite understanding this now, it took me a while to connect my observations in nursing school to the broader relevance of these principles across all living organisms. Just as animals can contract diseases in the wild, house plants can also suffer from ailments right in people's homes.

Just as trees can suffer from diseases right in people's backyards—so to speak—organizations are certainly not immune. The impact of disease on an organization, especially infectious diseases, can be particularly severe, potentially creating an outbreak that is difficult to remediate or eradicate without incurring serious damage and significant costs. The same principle applies to slowing the effects of the disease, giving both the organization and the organism a chance to fight it off.

Just as a healthy lifestyle can help prevent disease in a human organism, a healthy organizational culture can help prevent the negative impact of disease on an organization. This means fostering a culture where people believe in leadership through transparency, open communication, diversity, and a shared understanding of how to achieve goals and milestones. By promoting open communication, an organization can prevent the spread of rumors, negative attitudes, and misinformation.

Prioritizing diversity ensures a range of skill sets and perspectives, enabling the organization to adapt and innovate. Additionally, the company should reflect its customer base from the boardroom to its front-line employees.

By prioritizing the well-being of its employees and creating a safe work environment, an organization can mitigate the negative effects of physiological or psychological issues on its workforce.

Many preventive measures to avoid physical harm can be addressed more easily. In contrast, cultivating a psychologically safe work environment requires careful attention, purposefulness, and planning.

By staying properly hydrated—much like effective communication—we can slow down the aging process in organizations and prolong a disease-free lifespan, ultimately improving quality of life and reducing remediation costs.

Speaking of quality of life, we all expect that as we gain experience and age, life should improve. However, this expectation comes with its own concerns and challenges. Aging often increases susceptibility to disease.

Disease is progressive and can often be treated or remediated, just as it affects organizations. Unfortunately, in some cases, by the time the disease is recognized, it may be too late for the organism or organization to recover.

This is why as a leader it is imperative to know the pulse of your business—the pulse of your culture, the pulse of your people, and ultimately the pulse of how well the system is functioning and how healthy it is.

We also covered a bit about leadership. Much more of that is in the thought leaders section. **However, leadership, when broken down into its parts, has a common thread of influence. Employees grant this influence when there is trust. This trust becomes evident when leaders display the best intentions that provide value to the workforce and to the customers.**

Finally, I want to emphasize, for your consideration, stratified systems theory. I've spent a significant part of my post-collegiate adult life thinking about people, systems, and communication. This has led me to read hundreds of books and conduct deep dives into studies, all in search of the best systems and training methods. My quest has been to identify practices and methods that consistently produce the proposed results over time. Unfortunately, most systems are rigid, and their outcomes are not reliable. This means they cannot be repeated in similar circumstances. I urge you once again to consider utilizing stratified systems theory, emphasizing that there is no benefit to me if you do. The potential benefits for you and your organization are immense—especially if you're not on the partial list presented in this book or the longer list of companies already engaged in stabilizing and growing their organization.

Additionally, stratified systems theory boasts an impressive 96% accuracy rate.

To provide context for my insistence, I want to share my experience with Dr. Elliott Jacques. When I met him, he was 84 years old and just beginning to share his 40-plus years of research, trying to capture people's attention. Unfortunately, the magic of his age and the challenges of accepting and incorporating a new paradigm as we've discussed limited his ability to share his work fully in the time he had left.

I witnessed the effectiveness of his approach firsthand; I even tried to disrupt the process, yet it still delivered results. In each instance, SST aligned with the accuracy it proposed. I have also seen it work in several organizations on the short list. At the very least, I strongly encourage you to explore it for yourself and form your own opinion, rather than doing nothing and risking the consequences of a poor management structure that could jeopardize your legacy and your company.

As mentioned earlier, the people, culture, and maintenance of a learning culture are crucial to the best intentions within an organization. Just like a living organism, an organization thrives when its cells (employees) are synchronized and focused on preserving and enhancing it. When the culture of an organization is balanced, like healthy blood of an organism is in homeostasis—functioning well at any given moment—the organization can thrive and grow. When a learning culture is prevalent and active, the organization can innovate and adapt to the various challenges presented by changes in economics, customer demand, and even natural disasters like hurricanes, pandemics, floods, etc.. Ultimately, your managers will either sustain the effort or they will not.

Want a quick Organizational Health Check? Scan the QR code below for a special Biological Audit Framework Intro (BA Framework)

CHAPTER EIGHT

REMEDIATION AND REHABILITATION— HOW BIOLOGY THRIVES

In today's dynamic and rapidly changing business environment, it is essential for organizations to be adaptable and responsive to meet the evolving needs of their customers. To achieve this, companies must address multiple areas of their business, including culture, information sharing and training, management, security policies, customer value delivery, goal interpretation by the CEO (strategy, vision, charisma, trust, transparency, engagement, and feedback loops with employees), waste in processes, personnel, system flow (small intestine awareness), and the organization as a whole.

We have examined the key challenges organizations face in these areas and proposed solutions to address them. This includes prioritizing people, leveraging agile ways of working, applying lean thinking, utilizing the Awareness-Desir e-Knowledge-Ability-Reinforcement (ADKAR) change management method or a change management system that produces consistent results, ensuring true communication, and managing ego in management. Here, we will explore specific issues and solutions related to the organism-organization parallel.

Culture (Heart)

Problem: Many organizations struggle to build a positive and productive culture that fosters innovation, creativity, and teamwork. Often, employees feel disengaged and disconnected from the company's values and vision, leading to poor performance and high turnover rates.

Solution: To address this challenge, organizations must invest in creating a strong culture that aligns with their values and vision. This can be achieved by promoting transparency, trust, and collaboration, while providing opportunities for employee growth (a learning culture) and development. Recognizing and rewarding highly-performing employees is also essential. For example, companies like Google, SaaS, and Red Hat offer their employees a range of benefits and perks, including flexible working hours, discounted meals, onsite childcare, and healthcare services. These initiatives create a positive work environment and boost employee morale, making employees feel cared for and reducing stress related to basic needs like food and childcare. Leaders understand that prioritizing people is key.

An example of how culture impacts the working environment comes from a company in the finance and banking sector that serves the merger and acquisition industry. In a meeting with a potential customer, the lead manager made a joke about bringing along a "newbie to take notes." This particular employee had excelled academically at a prestigious university and athletically as a team captain, was now demonstrating his capability to learn quickly and apply that knowledge. He shared that his supervisor would often not communicate with him all day, sending assignments in the evening with the expectation of a response before meetings the next morning. When he was asked about the general culture, he mentioned that others experienced the same rigor and that same lack of communication, and no one liked it. This culture, where employees were told what to do without the freedom to think and perform, led to one result: attrition.

That employee, a potential rock star, and others have left the company since that interview. People want to be valued and need to find meaning, autonomy, and purpose in their work.

Lastly, it's important to consider the three levels that need to be addressed when we speak of culture:

1. The Business: Operational advancements can create strategic opportunities, influencing company culture and decisions. For instance, collaborations with industry leaders and acquisitions can transform a company's perception and offerings, enriching customer experiences and reinforcing employee engagement.

2. Management/Leadership: Key management processes directly shape organizational culture. Decisions regarding leadership appointments, recruitment strategies, and performance evaluations play pivotal roles. For example, at one well-known international music/podcast streaming company, their policies promoting accountability and trust, along with management practices that emphasize the recruitment of exceptional talent and fostering real, candid

feedback, contribute significantly to cultivating a vibrant organizational culture.

At this company, culture is talked about, acknowledged and is not developed by a canned approach or program, or is worked on secretly with the hope that employees will adapt or somehow magically think it is the best place in which to work. It is overt and inclusive.

3. People: People-centered strategies are crucial in shaping organizational culture. Initiatives such as starting performance management meetings with discussions about people and organizational issues emphasize a culture that prioritizes employee well-being and engagement. These approaches underscore the importance of people and foster a supportive and engaged environment.

Information Sharing and Training—Learning Culture (Lungs)

Problem: Many organizations struggle to share information and knowledge effectively across different teams and departments, leading to silos and duplication of effort. Additionally, many lack a culture of continuous learning and development, which can—and most likely will—impede their ability to adapt to new challenges and opportunities.

Solution: To address this challenge, organizations need to invest in building a culture of collaboration and knowledge sharing, leveraging tools and technologies such as collaboration platforms and social media. They should also provide regular training and development opportunities to enhance employees' skills and keep them up to date with the latest industry trends and best practices. For example, LinkedIn, SAP, Spotify, and countless other transformative companies offer their employees a range of online learning courses and development programs. They also allow time for employees to engage in learning, emphasizing its importance through management support. As a result, employees recognize the value of upskilling.

The transformation to a learning culture is exemplified by the company Adobe. Adobe opened a learning fund for its employees, which has significantly impacted their development. One indication of this cultural shift is the number of employees who have completed degrees, earned advanced technological certificates, and attended thousands of classes—many of whom still work for Adobe. In this learning culture, employees feel empowered to turn their aspirations into reality and manage their careers more effectively. By embracing the "creator economy," Adobe has positioned itself to rebound from the investor slowdown caused by the pandemic. Employees understand that continuous learning is key to staying ahead of customer demand and adapting to changing times.

Management—Frozen Layer: Incompetence and Screening of Information (Liver)

Problem: Many organizations struggle with ineffective management practices, resulting in poor and slow decision-making, as well as a lack of accountability. Additionally, many managers lack the necessary skills and expertise to lead their teams effectively, leading to low morale and high turnover rates. Often, this stems from the complexity of mental processing.

Solution: To address this challenge, organizations need to invest in building strong leadership capabilities at all levels. They should provide training and development opportunities for managers to enhance their skills and knowledge, while also fostering a culture of accountability and ownership. Furthermore, when given the opportunity to replace a manager, it's crucial to select the right candidate. Avoid choosing someone merely based on familiarity or convenience. Do not choose someone merely for their loyalty to the company, or because they have a great personality and are well-liked, unless they also possess the right complexity of mental processing. (Refer to the partial list at the end of this chapter on businesses that recognize the value of the right manager and/or leadership based on Dr. Jacques's work with stratified systems theory and ask yourself why your organization isn't on that list.)

When it comes to leadership and management, companies should leverage tools and technologies such as data analytics and performance metrics to make more informed, data-driven decisions. For example, Amazon employs a data-driven approach to decision-making, utilizing its vast data resources to inform its business strategy and operations. Similarly, companies like Verizon, H.J. Heinz, Shell Oil, and Johnson & Johnson use data effectively while ensuring they have the right capabilities and management practices in place.

Security Policies (Physical and Technological), Operations, and How We Provide Value to Customers (Skin and Muscles)

Problem: Many organizations struggle to ensure the security of their data and systems, leading to data breaches and other security incidents. Additionally, many organizations find it challenging to provide value to their customers, resulting in poor customer satisfaction and low brand loyalty.

Solution: To address these challenges, organizations need to invest in building robust security policies and protocols to protect their data and systems from cyber threats, both internally and externally. They should also prioritize customer-centricity, ensuring that their operations consistently deliver value to their customer leveraging customer feedback and insights to inform their product development and marketing strategies. For example, Apple is known for its strong focus on customer experience, design, and feedback loops, which has helped it build a loyal customer base and a strong brand identity. This emphasis on security is also highly valued by Apple users, as reflected in user feedback surveys and Net Promoter Scores.

Another significant example is the 2017 data breach at Equifax, a large U.S.-based credit reporting company, which affected approximately 143 million Americans. The breach was caused by an unpatched vulnerability in the company's website software. Equifax faced criticism for its slow response to the breach, and its initial attempts to remedy the situation were perceived as inadequate. As a result, the company's reputation suffered significantly, leading to multiple lawsuits and investigations.

To prevent similar incidents, companies can implement lean thinking principles to enhance their cybersecurity posture. By streamlining security policies, procedures, and workflows, they can minimize waste while maximizing value to the customer. Adopting agile ways of working allows organizations to respond more quickly to emerging threats and vulnerabilities, helping them stay ahead of potential attackers.

In addition to cybersecurity, companies must focus on how they provide value to their customers. They should establish policies that ensure their products and services meet or exceed customer expectations.

For example, in 2013, Target suffered a massive data breach that exposed the personal and financial information of over 110 million customers. The breach resulted from a vulnerability in the company's point-of-sale systems, which were not properly secured. Target faced heavy criticism for its handling of the breach and its failure to protect customer data, which led to customer anger and lost revenue. Simply put, this breach did not meet or exceed customer expectations.

To prevent similar incidents, companies should prioritize the development of secure products, ensure robust security for all services, and adopt lean operations that facilitate a continuous flow of value. This can be achieved by implementing the principles of lean thinking and agile practices. By focusing on the uninterrupted delivery of value to the customer, companies can prioritize the development of secure, high-quality products and services. A customer-centric approach ensures that organizations meet customer needs and provide value at every stage of the process.

The analogy between the human organism and business systems illustrates the importance of a continuous flow of value to the customer, leading to faster market delivery, increased customer satisfaction, and stronger long-term relationships. This also implies the absence of organizational silos, which does not mean eliminating departments or divisions. Instead, it means using the structure of hierarchical systems as intended, rather than how they have often evolved.

Finally, the entire system within the organism illustrates how different parts of a business work together to create a continuous flow of value to the customer. To achieve this, companies must adopt an integrated approach, focusing on collaboration, transparency, integrity, protection, and feedback.

A pertinent example of the need for effective product development, security to ensure customer value and quality, and operations—often referred to as DevSecOps—can be seen in the Volkswagen (VW) emissions scandal, also known as Dieselgate. This major controversy emerged in 2015 when it was revealed that VW had intentionally installed software in their diesel engines that detected when the car was being tested for emissions and adjusted performance to comply with regulations. However, during normal driving conditions, the engines emitted up to forty times the legal limit of nitrogen oxides (NOx), harmful pollutants that contribute to respiratory illnesses and smog.

The scandal had far-reaching consequences for VW, the wider automotive industry, and public health and the environment. VW eventually admitted to installing defeat devices in eleven million vehicles worldwide, including around five hundred thousand in the United States. The company faced numerous lawsuits, fines, and investigations, ultimately agreeing to pay over $30 billion in settlements, penalties, and buybacks.

The scandal exposed a culture of dishonesty and unethical behavior within VW, where executives and engineers prioritized profits and market share over compliance, environmental responsibility, and ethical customer satisfaction.

The company's management and leadership faced criticism for failing to cultivate a culture of transparency and accountability, allowing the use of illegal software to go unchecked for years, despite its known existence.

In the aftermath of the scandal, VW pledged to overhaul its corporate governance and compliance practices and to invest heavily in electric vehicles and other forms of sustainable mobility. The incident served as a stark reminder of the importance of ethical behavior, transparency, and accountability in business, highlighting the risks and consequences of failing to uphold these values. The integration of development, security, and operations is essential, as these elements should function as checks and balances for one another.

To prevent similar incidents, companies must adopt a holistic approach that emphasizes collaboration and transparency. By embracing agile methodologies and lean thinking principles, organizations can foster an environment where employees feel empowered to share their ideas and provide feedback on company processes and ethical behaviors. By cultivating a culture of trust, accountability, collaboration, transparency, integrity, and feedback, companies can ensure they are working together to create a continuous flow of value for customers.

Brain (Strategy, Vision, Charisma, Trust, Transparency, Engagement, Feedback Loop to and from Employees)

Problem: Many organizations struggle to develop a clear and compelling vision and strategy, which can impede their ability to achieve their goals and objectives. Additionally, they often face challenges in building trust and engagement among employees, resulting in low morale, disengagement, high attrition, and generally dissatisfied employees—many of whom may never voice their concerns, especially if they fear retribution for being transparent or believe they will be ignored anyway.

Solution: To address this challenge, organizations need to invest in developing a clear and compelling vision and strategy that aligns with their values and mission. This vision must be simplified and effectively communicated by managers (supervisors, leads, etc.). Additionally, organizations should prioritize building trust and engagement with their employees, leveraging communication and feedback mechanisms to keep everyone informed and involved.

For example, OOFOS, a leading online retailer, is renowned for its strong focus on company culture and employee engagement, which has helped it cultivate a loyal customer base and a robust brand identity.

The leadership is so committed to this that when you call the company after hours, the voice you hear on the recording welcoming you and providing options is that of the CEO. Look them up and call after hours to experience it for yourself. This is leadership in action—where the company practices what it preaches, rather than simply stating ideals.

In my early days as a consultant, I had the opportunity to work as a proxy for a large U.S. telecommunications company. While at the corporate office, I attended a company-wide meeting with over a thousand attendees. At the end of the meeting, the CEO of this company, which employs more than one hundred thousand people, stayed for an hour with a notebook and pen, allowing employees to stand in line to share their thoughts and provide feedback.

By doing so, he realized amongst other things, that employees often had to leave campus to get certain drinks, especially "good" coffee. Within thirty days, plans were underway for two on-campus coffee shops, complete with snacks, coolers of water, and other drinks on every other floor. Fast forward one year: not only was there massive gratitude for these changes, but he received many a thank-you, for just taking the time to listen to the employees. This is how effective feedback loops can work.

Small Intestines (Waste in Processes, Personnel, System Flow)

Problem: Many organizations struggle with inefficiencies in their processes, resulting in waste and duplication of effort. These inefficiencies often lead to a blame game that no one enjoys, creating silos as people hesitate to collaborate for fear of being blamed. This dynamic also leads to deviations from established norms or standards, as employees alter their work processes in an attempt to avoid blame, mistakenly believing they are improving efficiency. As a result, there is a critical need for standardized systems and possibly an overhaul. Additionally, many organizations struggle with managing personnel effectively, resulting in poor performance and high turnover rates.

Solution: To address these challenges, organizations should adopt lean thinking principles, which prioritize continuous improvement and waste reduction. They should invest in process automation and optimization where appropriate, leveraging tools and technologies such as robotic process automation (RPA) and business process management (BPM) software. Examining value streams will help identify where services and products are being affected by multiple teams or individuals from different teams or divisions.

Observing these touchpoints helps define and design the way business should be conducted. Additionally, organizations should prioritize personnel management by providing regular feedback and development opportunities to enhance employee skills and performance. For example, Toyota is renowned for its focus on lean thinking and continuous improvement, which has made it one of the most efficient and successful automotive manufacturers in the world.

Want proof? Toyota is considered one of the world's largest automakers, and its performance has remained strong over the past five years. Here are some key performance indicators:

- ○ Revenue: Toyota's revenue has consistently increased over the last five years. In the fiscal year ending March 2022, Toyota's consolidated revenue was 31.6 trillion yen, up from 29.9 trillion yen in the previous fiscal year.
- ○ Net Income: Toyota has also posted strong net income figures consistently. In the fiscal year ending March 2022, Toyota's consolidated net income was 2.4 trillion yen, up from 2.1 trillion yen in the previous fiscal year.
- ○ Sales Volume: Toyota has maintained its position as the world's leading automaker in terms of sales volume. In 2021, Toyota sold 7.6 million vehicles globally, up from 7.2 million in 2017.
- ○ Market Share: Toyota's market share has remained robust, especially in its home market of Japan. In 2021,

Toyota held a 31.3 percent market share in Japan, up from 29.6 percent in 2017.

○ Innovation: Toyota has been investing heavily in new technologies, such as electric and autonomous vehicles. The company has also expanded its product lineup with the introduction of several new models.

Overall, Toyota has performed exceptionally well over the last five years, showcasing strong financial performance, high sales volume, and a continued commitment to innovation. There is a direct correlation between these successes and the principles of lean thinking and continuous improvement.

The Entire System in an Organism Compared to Business Systems (Human Organism Working Together) Continuous Flow of Value to the Customer, Faster to Market, Customer Satisfaction, Long-Term Relationships

Problem: Many organizations struggle to achieve a continuous flow of value to their customers, resulting in slow time to market and poor customer satisfaction. Additionally, many organizations find it challenging to build long-term relationships with their customers, leading to low brand loyalty and high customer churn. Often, when a company is struggling, it tends to appear disjointed and operates in an uncoordinated manner, affecting the smooth delivery of its products and services. This situation can be especially detrimental for veteran companies.

Solution: To address this challenge, organizations need to adopt agile ways of working that prioritize collaboration, continuous improvement, and customer-centricity. They should also leverage tools and technologies such as DevSecOps to enhance their operational efficiency and continuous integration/

continuous delivery (CI/CD) pipelines to enable faster time to market and higher-quality products. It's important to note that DevSecOps is not just for software companies.

Agile methodologies and CI/CD practices have been adopted across various manufacturing and service-oriented companies.

Additionally, organizations should prioritize building long-term relationships with their customers by leveraging feedback and insights to inform their product development and marketing strategies. For example, Spotify is renowned for its agile approach and customer-centric culture, which have propelled it to become one of the most successful music streaming platforms in the world.

Organizations face multiple challenges in building a strong and sustainable business, including culture, information sharing and training, management, security policies, and how they provide value to customers. These elements represent the brain, small intestines, and entire system of an organization compared to business systems. By adopting agile practices, lean thinking, stratified systems theory, requisite organization principles, effective consulting (not just any consultant, as many fall short, especially those from the big four), and ADKAR change management principles, organizations can tackle these challenges.

This approach fosters a culture of continuous improvement, collaboration, engaged employees, learning, innovation, and customer-centricity, enabling them to thrive in today's dynamic and rapidly changing business environment.

Yes, all of these elements together—THIS WILL TAKE MASSIVE COORDINATION AND COMMUNICATION (more communication than coordination).

In this final example, we will see how crucial it is to structure a company with the right people in the right positions and to manage change elements effectively in order to achieve outstanding results:

A major company in a $100 billion industry opted to bring in a new leader. Instead of outsourcing this effort to a consulting firm, the board chose to interview potential candidates alongside a stratified systems theory consultant. The interviews were recorded and analyzed. After selecting the right person, the new leader understood the results of his interview process and applied the same method to assess his top leaders. Some managers were reassigned to different responsibilities, while others received severance packages.

After a year, the management team was restructured and already facilitating change. Part of this transformation involved devolving decision-making authority to the knowledge workers—those closest to the customer—who can provide what customers need and want. This shift occurred because managers at the appropriate level of responsibility for their complexity of mental processing (CMP) do not have to rely on ego for their success.

One reason this company is thriving is that it made a one-time investment in developing effective leadership and management practices, some based on natural laws, which prioritize collaboration, communication, and accountability.

They fostered a culture of trust and transparency, empowering employees to take ownership of their work and rewarding their contributions. A similar example is IBM, which implemented a comprehensive leadership development program focused on building effective management skills and practices.

As mentioned in earlier chapters, here is the partial requisite organization list of which I have asked you to consider getting on it if you're not on it yet.

REQUISITE ORGANIZATIONS— STRATIFIED SYSTEMS THEORY PARTIAL LIST

RBC Centura Bank of Montreal
Mechanics & Farmers Bank
Ashland Chemical Company
Mallinckrodt Specialty Chemical
Shell Chemical Company
SAP AG, Avery Dennison
H. J. Heinz
Alcoa
GlaxoSmithKline
Johnson and Johnson
State of North Carolina Rex Hospital
CGU Insurance Verizon Inc.
American Society of Training and Development
CPS Energy

GATEWAYS TO ENHANCED MINDFULNESS

In the world of organizational development, numerous ideas and theories are available for consideration, but not all of them hold value. Some lack depth and experience, rendering them ineffective, while others are merely novel concepts without practical application. As a thought leader, it is crucial to sift through the abundance of material and identify ideas that genuinely offer value.

This supplementary content explores the concept of liminality, which pertains to the spaces between moments. Often overlooked, these interstitial spaces present ample opportunities for feedback and learning that can greatly benefit individuals and organizations attentive to them.

Undoubtedly, there are countless opportunities to gain experience from liminality, as it manifests nearly a hundred thousand times each day. I will guide you through several Gateways to Enhanced Mindfulness (GEMs) that arise during these liminal moments. These GEMs enable you to make significant strides in your personal and organizational growth toward becoming the best version of your leadership self, even if you do not currently hold a formal leadership position.

The Power of Liminality

Liminality represents the transitional space between moments, where feedback emerges. Every action we take and every thought we have generates a reaction. When we interact with others or systems, these actions produce outcomes. Amidst these moments, we often rush ahead to the next point, overlooking many of the most impactful experiences. While subtle, these moments harbor our most valuable lessons.

One key to maximizing these moments is to consciously acknowledge them. By recognizing their occurrence and understanding their messages, we can expedite our learning process and enhance our decision-making abilities. For instance, imagine you are engaged in a conversation with colleagues, and someone mentions a topic unfamiliar to you. In the space between their comment and your response, you have an opportunity to reflect on why you lack knowledge about the topic and how you can proactively learn more if it holds significance.

Real-World Feedback

Liminality is full of real-world behaviors and outcomes. By becoming a student of liminality, we can begin to notice these moments and learn from them. For example, in a conversation with a couple of business owners, the topic of music came up. One person mentioned a song, which led to a discussion about the band's history. In the space between conversational exchanges, there lies a wealth of insight waiting to be discovered.

In this particular conversation in between comments, I realized that my response was not relevant to the conversation and added no value. In reflecting on this, I had to ask myself why I responded that way and whether I was being authentic and genuine in the discussion. As he spoke about the names of people I didn't know and how they could have survived as a band if they had gotten along, I found myself in a moment of complete unfamiliarity. I was not interested in the details and awkwardly looked at the speaker as he sought confirmation that I was following the conversation. I said, "I like their music," which had nothing to do with the topic at hand. I briefly wondered if I was pacifying him or feeling empathy—perhaps even sympathy—because I really didn't care. In my quest to be authentic and genuine in my communication, I would have been better served just to nod and continue listening.

The Importance of Distractions

Leaders often overlook the value of liminality due to distractions. While some distractions can be valuable, the ideas presented here have stood the test of time. By becoming a student of liminality, leaders can improve their communication, feedback, and decision-making skills, leaving behind a lasting legacy. When it comes to distractions, I was once asked about inertia and whether distractions are the killers of inertia. My answer was yes if a human being initiated the inertia to achieve a task.

The GEM related to distraction is to recognize what they are. I worked for a company that used Microsoft's default browsers. It took me a while to figure out that when the default browser opened, there were enough stories to keep me occupied for days—or, as Joey "Carmels" Rodriguez, an author, musician and performer referred to it as, another "deep rabbit hole."

I found myself fifteen stories deep in twenty tabs across the browser, all interesting but none helping me complete the work on which I was previously focused. After wasting immense amounts of time reading through useless stories and news bites, I became aware of this distraction. The next few times I needed the browser, I was careful not to click a single news bite, thus avoiding the deep rabbit hole.

Knowing what constitutes a distraction and not engaging with it is key to staying focused. Unfortunately, we all face distractions, and how we deal with them is crucial. During one of my coaching sessions with Joey, we discovered a critical structure related to distraction. He is in the process of sharing what he uncovered, and my interpretation of that discovery is that distractions can develop you, destroy you, or even define you. Perhaps he will call it The Four D's of Paying Attention.

Another critical GEM is the idea that what we see is not always reality. As humans, we are neurologically wired in similar ways, but we all have scotomas—blind spots that limit our thinking, imagination, and behavior. These blind spots can be particularly limiting when it comes to decision-making, as we may act on significant implications without fully understanding them or relying solely on someone else's word about the information we should know.

To overcome these limitations, we must actively seek out and learn more about what we do not know, remaining open to seeing things in a new light. The truth is it is amazing what we fail to see in familiar environments. To illustrate this point, consider the following example: In a seminar, participants are shown a shape containing words and are asked to read the four words within 10 seconds. Despite repeated exposure to the same image throughout the day, many participants fail to see the four words that are actually there, even though others who spot the unique wording read it aloud when asked. Most people only see three words.

We have spent hours in training before all participants realize what is really there. They see what they want to see due to their own unique coding and familiarity. As a result, they miss the details of what is present and do not understand it until it is pointed out and made explicit to them. This exercise highlights how blind spots can limit our perception and decision-making abilities, underscoring the importance of seeking new perspectives and challenging our assumptions.

Interestingly, I have used this same image for over twenty-five years in training with the same results.

Avoiding these blind spots is not difficult; it simply requires asking the right questions, testing your assumptions, and then acting.

By becoming a student of these GEMs, we can gain a deeper understanding of ourselves, our interactions, and our decision-making processes.

The art of leadership is a multifaceted and challenging endeavor. Whether taking over or starting a business, the uncertainty of predicting outcomes can be daunting, with many factors to consider, from market pressures to regulations and workforce concerns. As a leader, it is crucial to understand the value of seeking knowledge from those around you—the janitor, a team employee, or anyone else in the company who could offer invaluable insights that can be learned in an hour of passionate teaching rather than a full day's class. It's important to be aware of your patterns in this area and take action when you catch yourself overlooking the wisdom of those around you.

Another GEM in the world of thought leadership is the need to think differently.

It's crucial to break free from the constraints of dualistic thinking, where everything is either black or white, up or down, and embrace the concept that both sides exist simultaneously. When we can accept this, we can make innovative decisions without the fear of the opposite occurring, as it remains a possibility. Recognizing this gives us the opportunity to focus on growth—whether in market share, employee engagement, or customer satisfaction. (The Second Law of Psychology states, "what you focus on grows.") The first key insight is: "you get more of what you reinforce."

Acceptance of duality doesn't imply a lack of commitment; rather, it allows you to focus on what you want instead of what you do not want.

Leaders must recognize the need for balance, understanding that while change is necessary, stability is also important. As humans, we are hardwired to think a certain way, with our neurological makeup influencing how we perceive the world. Traditional theories of psychology can be complex and overwhelming, highlighting the need for simpler explanations to understand our thought patterns.

It is essential to recognize our blind spots—those areas where we don't know what we don't know—that limit our thinking, behavior, and imagination.

When we can acknowledge these blind spots, we begin to make strides toward becoming the best version of ourselves. Running a successful business requires a delicate balance of planning and flexibility. As a business leader, you need to understand that success and failure are two sides of the same coin. To truly succeed, you must accept the duality of business life and cultivate a mindset of resilience and growth. You must be prepared for the risks and uncertainties that come with running a business and remain adaptable when faced with unexpected challenges.

One of the most important aspects of building a successful business is understanding the importance of continuous effort, direction, and evolution. Rather than focusing solely on milestones or target states, you must emphasize the ongoing process of building and growing your business. This requires a constant awareness of value plateaus and the need to make changes that enhance the flow and value proposition of your products and services.

This leads to a key GEM that is often overlooked: the value of linguistics—both receptive and expressive, and not just spoken. It's not just what you communicate that matters, but how you communicate it. The way you make initial contact with someone can significantly impact your ability to build rapport and trust. By understanding the three main representational systems and learning how to communicate effectively, you can establish a strong foundation of leadership rooted in trust.

As you embark on your journey as a business leader, remember that there is no clear destination or endpoint. Running a business is more akin to creating music than achieving a specific goal. The focus should always be on the continuous effort, direction, and evolution of the business. By embracing the duality of business life, accepting risks and uncertainties, and prioritizing continuous growth and development, you can build a successful business that stands the test of time.

Whether you're starting a new business or taking over an existing one, you are likely to feel a sense of energy and confidence in your ability to make the business successful. After all, you have experience and skills to draw upon to help you reach your goals. However, as with many things in life, running a business is not a straightforward path. In fact, it's more like creating music than reaching a specific endpoint. There is no clear destination in business—no final goal to be attained. Rather, successful businesses require constant effort, direction, and evolution to exist and thrive.

Consider this: in music, there is no destination, and the point is never simply the end. If it were, the music that reached the conclusion the fastest would be considered the best. But this isn't the case. Similarly, in business, focusing solely on milestones or target states can be limiting. Instead, the emphasis should be on the continuous evolution of the workforce's ability to learn, improve, and adapt the business. As a business leader, you must consider these aspects concurrently.

This means that while a manager, CEO, or team works on the cascaded and translated goals or objectives from the CEO, leadership must continuously understand and plan for the plateaus in value where changes can be made to enhance performance.

Only the flow but also the value proposition of new products, add-ons, or other variations—including services—can be enhanced by these plateaus. Although you won't see them marked on a calendar, these are simply points where teams can come together, gather their resources, and confirm what they need and want to achieve in the next iteration of work before launching. These continuously occurring markers determine whether the work is, on course, effective, and desired by customers.

The notion that the true value of expressed and received linguistics (a form of communication) lies solely in what we communicate is simply not true. My first round of collegiate learning yielded a degree in speech, hearing, and language science with a minor in engineering. From both communication and engineering perspectives, the emphasis was often on the specifics and formatting of what is being shared, which focuses more on the "how" than on the "what."

As a former healthcare leader, I learned that the most important thing I could do when engaging someone—whether in therapy, which I practiced for several years early in my career, or when interacting with groups—was to make initial contact and make it count. In my opinion, this aligns with the saying, "You only have one chance to make a first impression." This raises the question: Is this the best way to focus on communication, especially if there will be future interactions?

What if the intent of your initial contact was to understand where someone is, related to the three main representational systems? In this way you know along with them, <u>how to communicate best to them.</u>

These systems are key to communication and rapport, serving as the foundation from which trust is built. Up to this point in the book, I have consistently suggested that you engage with people to understand them—learning how they think, how they feel, how they perceive the world, and what captures their attention in the company. This is why this particular GEM is critical to building a strong foundation of leadership: it's not just about what you communicate, but how you communicate it. If people don't understand what you are saying, then what is the point?

Communication is ineffective if it lacks consistency; this may be the final conclusion on the subject: CONSISTENCY!

Communication is an essential part of our everyday lives, and the way we communicate significantly impacts our ability to build relationships and trust with others. One critical aspect of effective communication is understanding the three primary representational systems: visual, auditory, and kinesthetic (VAK) modalities.

These systems are crucial because they reflect the different ways we express and receive information, both from within ourselves and from external sources. The representational system we use can vary based on our experiences and cultural backgrounds, leading to gaps and misunderstandings between primary and secondary representations.

To overcome these differences, it is essential to learn how to observantly interact with others. Eye movements are a valuable tool for determining which representational system a person is using.

By paying attention to whether someone's eyes move left or right, or up or down, we can better understand which mode of communication someone is using—whether visual or auditory.

While understanding these representational systems is critical, it is equally important to be cautious when interpreting what someone is saying. Words carry different meanings and relevance for different people based on their experiences and backgrounds. Therefore, it's essential to consider the context in which words are used and how they relate to a person's experiences.

Effective communication requires a deeper understanding of the various ways we express and receive information. By paying attention to representational systems and observing eye movements, we can connect more effectively with others and build stronger relationships.

However, we must remember that words can mean different things to different people, so we should be careful in our interpretations.

The world we live in is often shaped by our beliefs rather than objective truths. In this GEM, I urge you to set aside scientific proof and personal beliefs to explore and practice the power of representational systems in communication. By identifying a person's lead modality—visual, auditory, or kinesthetic—you can present information in a way that resonates with their specific representational system. This approach not only makes communication more effective but also fosters deeper rapport and trust. Imagine someone saying to you, "Now you're speaking my language." This connection can occur in spoken conversations, sign language, written forms, braille, and even through body language in moments of deep rapport.

To test for each modality, ask questions that guide the participant's representational system. For instance, visual questions might inquire about the color of a particular house, the pattern on a known building, or what they see when they first enter their home after work. Auditory questions could ask about their favorite sound in nature or the noise of a car that won't start. Kinesthetic questions might involve the feeling of stepping into water or the sensation of transitioning from a hot shower into a bathroom left open in the middle of winter.

As you pose these questions, pay attention to shifts in the participant's eye movements. These shifts indicate changes in their representational system and allow you to tailor your communication to their modality.

This skill is essential in business settings, where connecting with your audience and building trust are critical for success— especially in sales.

Remember, the power of representational systems lies in the ability to communicate in a way that resonates with the other person's experience. It's not about convincing them to see things your way; rather, it's about creating a space for effective communication and building stronger relationships.

Rapport building is a crucial aspect of effective communication, and there's yet another GEM that can help us forge even stronger connections with others. This GEM involves shadowing and reflecting the behavior and communication styles of others. As social beings, we tend to gravitate toward those who are similar to us, making shadowing and reflecting incredibly powerful tools for building rapport. I have witnessed this during my travels around the world. It's fascinating how two people can find themselves at a conference abroad or far from home often find others from their same area and tend to spend more time together. This connection happens regardless of titles, skin color, hierarchy, or job types. Let's delve deeper.

According to research, words account for only about 7 percent of our communication, while tone contributes approximately 38 percent, and body language represents nearly 55 percent. This means our postures and tone significantly impact how we communicate and the messages we convey. Our bodies must move to express emotion, and certain postures can evoke feelings such as boldness, fear, worry, gratitude, happiness, and anger. By observing the postures and tonality of others and mirroring them, we can create a sense of familiarity and comfort, leading to stronger connections.

In one seminar, a CFO from a well-known mid-size company admitted to struggling with knowing whether people were engaged and listening during his presentations at company-wide meetings. After half a day in a Professional Communication for Leaders seminar, he stood and said to his peers, "Wow, I realized in the last few hours that I was very unaware of how I communicate and how important it is to understand what that means. I thought I was great at telling the truth and sharing valuable information that affected our employees and the future of our company, but my communication style was out of sync with most of them. It surely did not create trust or faith in my ability to make good financial decisions, despite the positive news."

It was apparent that the CFO's communication style did not align with the primary representational system of most participants. Most people are visual communicators, and by adjusting his communication style to include more visual references, the CFO was able to better connect with his audience and build rapport. (The CFO's primary communication modality was based on auditory representational styles.)

Communication must be consistent. In the business realm, we call it messaging. Messaging must be consistent and persistent. If a message is delivered at a one-time all-company meeting and is then hardly mentioned afterward, consider that a failure. If the first law of psychology is "you get more of what you reinforce," and the second is "you get more of what you focus on," then your messaging must be a focal point if you are serious about achieving results. Consistency is the most critical factor in communicating with the intent of eliciting a specific action or reaction. Messaging will determine the success or failure of any transformation effort, and how you say it will always be more important than what you say.

Just as communication is important, shadowing and reflecting the behavior and communication of others can be effective tools for building rapport. Adjusting our communication style to match the primary representational system of our audience can help us influence them and connect more easily.

The C-Level Trap

While C-level executives tend to think further ahead than most employees (CMP), true leadership requires the ability to integrate current progress into future increments of work toward a more impactful purpose.

This natural capability is often overlooked in succession planning, but it can help leaders consistently think about how to provide value to customers.

As a leader, it is vital to understand the compounding nature of business and the importance of incremental work toward a loftier purpose. C-level executives, in particular, are expected to possess a higher complexity of mental processing to integrate current progress into future increments of work toward that loftier purpose, which is a hallmark of true leadership, as stated in stratified systems theory.

Businesses operate in compounding incremental stages that should move progressively toward partial completion, similar to the stages of growth, digestion, and disease-fighting in the human body.

Unfortunately, many businesses fail to recognize this fact, and their inability to evolve and adapt ultimately leads to their downfall. Let me be clear: I'm not advocating for or against any specific project management tool or methodology. The facts are undeniable and have been for quite some time. If you have yet to realize the benefits of empowering your employees to be active participants in their work, streamline processes, enhance the quality of their products and services, and engage with customers in the process, then it's time to heed the warning bells. Do not wait any longer.

To overcome this trap, businesses must learn to operate fluidly and embrace the mindset of incremental work, allowing employees and managers to implement it while leaders focus on continuous improvement and the flow of value to customers. This requires a genuine connection to employees.

Leading to trust and influence enables employees to take full responsibility for the implementation of their work.

In everyday life, tunnel vision can prevent us from recognizing opportunities or potential threats that fall outside our usual focus. To counteract this, we must consciously broaden our awareness and consider more information, even if it seems irrelevant at first.

The implementation and continuous delivery of value, along with the ongoing improvement of the value delivery process, are critical to the success of operations. Leaders must focus on what matters and empower employees and managers to engage in incremental work aligned with the company's purpose while continuously enhancing the value delivery process.

Success requires constant effort, direction, and evolution to thrive. It's a delicate balance of planning and flexibility—accepting the potential for failure while striving to be a leader in the marketplace. This acceptance is key to consciously mitigating negative possibilities rather than fearfully avoiding them. It allows us to focus on doing our best, learning from our mistakes, and building strong relationships with stakeholders through transparency, honesty, and accountability.

As Napoleon Hill, the author of *Think and Grow Rich*, said, "Keep your mind on the things you want and off the things you don't want" (Hill, 1937).

Each advancement should occur incrementally, moving toward partial completion of work rather than immediately transitioning to the next stage. These stages and plateaus serve as launching points that require careful planning and execution for what comes next.

This is a continuous, never-ending process, and businesses that fail to recognize this fact are destined to fail. Companies must learn to operate in stages, constantly evolving and adapting to new challenges and opportunities. Incremental processes must become second nature for how employees work.

By working incrementally, employees—often referred to as knowledge workers—can take true responsibility for adapting to rapidly shifting customer needs. This approach brings the customer closer to the production or development process, allowing both employees and customers to collaborate in making adjustments to ensure the value delivered matches that for which the customer is willing to pay. This is the essence of customer satisfaction.

The ability to focus on what matters is critical. Just as in music, it's not the speed at which you reach the end that counts, but the continuous effort, direction, and evolution of the process. If speed were the sole measure of success, then the musician who finishes first would be deemed superior to slower counterparts. Leaders must consider both the implementation and continuous delivery of value, along with the ongoing improvement of the value delivery process, operating fluidly and consistently.

This approach involves planning for plateaus and launching from the preceding increment of work as part of the strategy. The key to success with incremental work is to empower employees to take full responsibility for making it work. This requires building genuine connections with employees, fostering moments when trust is established. Such connections lead to influence and, ultimately, complete trust.

When this is achieved, you will have reached a state of symbiotic balance that most leaders don't even realize exists.

As a business leader, the ability to remain calm during chaos is undeniably a critical trait. When faced with tough decisions that may create fear among employees, leaders must learn to stay levelheaded, avoiding reactive responses that stifle innovation and independent thinking. Research has shown that people often freeze in fear under stress, which can have dire consequences (Carmichael, 2019).

To maintain calm, one of the most important GEMs (Growth, Engagement, and Mindfulness) is the ability to categorize thoughts effectively. Our perceptions are often limited by our biases, making it essential to separate what we believe is happening from what is actually occurring (Covey, 1989). This is particularly important during moments of liminality, when our biology filters out more than it allows in, leaving us lacking the attention needed to excel in influence and succeed entrepreneurially.

For instance, consider the scenario of driving down the road and suddenly encountering a truck in your lane, forcing you to swerve and brake. Most people react emotionally in such situations, feeling angry or frustrated. However, this emotional reaction is driven by interpretation rather than facts. By choosing to focus solely on the facts (i.e., a truck entered the lane), one can avoid the emotional response and maintain control of the situation. This is not to say that embracing this GEM moment is easy; it requires commitment and practice to categorize your experiences through a factual lens. Yet over time, this approach allows you to reduce emotional biases and rely on your intuition. Emotions can serve as a confirming notion rather than a guiding template for business.

To succeed in both personal and professional settings, it is essential to expand our awareness by paying attention to details we might otherwise overlook. This requires intentional effort and practice. By observing our surroundings, honing our attention to detail, and developing our categorization skills, we can enhance our ability to make informed decisions and remain calm during moments of chaos.

Every interaction we have creates a feedback loop that is often overlooked. The communication model we discussed earlier—comprising 58 percent body language, 35 percent tone, and 7 percent words—is a critical component of this loop. This model explains why shadowing and reflecting techniques are so effective. When you observe a person's body language and tone, you gain valuable feedback that informs your communication and decision-making. In the new virtual workplace, if you implement a virtual or flexible policy, consider using a communication platform that encourages video interaction, allowing you to lead by example and promote the use of cameras.

However, it's not just about observation; it's also about how you use that information. The GEM lies in reflecting back to the other person what you observe in their body language, tone, and words. This practice helps build rapport and trust while reducing stress for both parties. By tuning in to these subtle cues, you gain a deeper understanding of how your own body is reacting, as well as the reactions of those around you.

As you put all the pieces together, you'll begin to see how everything fits into the bigger picture. Everything we've discussed in these eight chapters—from the importance of incremental workflows to the need for leadership to remain calm under pressure, from the power of perception and attention to the value of feedback loops—starts to make sense. As you implement changes in your organization that align with this understanding, you'll begin to earn trust, not blind loyalty, from both your employees and customers.

So, pay attention to the feedback loop and use the information you gather to improve your communication and decision-making. This small but powerful step can lead to a more successful and fulfilling business.

One of the final GEMs I want to introduce is a version of a cardiogram created by Robin Bittner, which can be adapted for businesses. This straightforward instrument has a tremendous impact when used correctly.

For teams producing services and products, it's essential to gauge how well, how fast, and how consistently they can deliver value without disruption to your customer base—both internally and externally. The primary benefit of this approach is that it allows leadership and teams to "predictively monitor" future work patterns based on current performance measured and analyzed over several incremental periods.

To briefly describe its functionality, we can draw a quick comparison to cardiogram results from the human heart.

The human heart is a miraculous organ, critical to our existence. We know so much about it that some theories even suggest that the heart has its own brain (Dr. Laurence Martel, 2003). Another well-known fact is that the heart functions on pulses generated by an electrical system unique to it. Because it is electrical—much like the systems in your home or office that power nearly everything—we should be able to measure the electricity from the heart's pulse. This is accomplished through an electrocardiogram, commonly known as an EKG, a term we will use from here on out.

You will see how incremental work, culture, pulse, feedback loops, monitoring (trust but verify), and many of the GEMs we covered earlier in the book come together through this simple system.

Ultimately, it can provide you with more information about how work is being produced in your organization than meetings, emails (unless they contain a business cardiogram), conference calls, and other methods of information sharing.

I will try to simplify the concept of the EKG, but please do not underestimate this GEM.

First, understand that the electrocardiogram serves to monitor how the heart is functioning. It specifically measures the frequency, rate, and rhythm of the heart. When the EKG is read or interpreted, the information gathered tells us how easily, normally, hard, or poorly the heart is working. In business, we refer to this as productivity, but that's not enough. We also need to assess how efficiently the heart is working and the quality of the work it produces.

Of course, this is directly correlated to the purpose of business: to deliver quality services and products that bring satisfaction to our customers. When your business can meet demand, cater to customer needs, and do so proficiently and efficiently, any business can thrive.

Here is a picture of how we get an EKG.

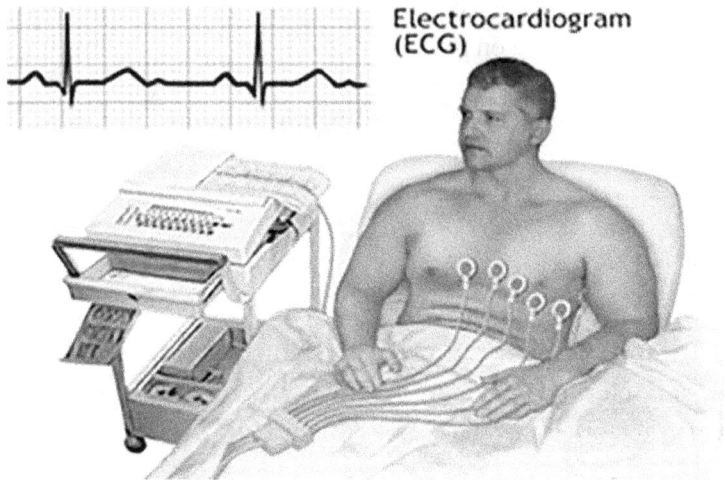

Figure 1 A.D.A.M.

Leads are placed on the patient. Here, "leads" refers not to employees but to leadership characteristics. A quick translation to business is that leads must embody every characteristic of effective leadership. This is not to say that employees also cannot be great leaders; however, based on everything we've discussed—whether we call it emotional intelligence (EQ) or pure leadership—the term that best defines how we achieve work in the human organism is LEADS.

I recently had a conversation with my brother Steve, who has been in cybersecurity for more than thirty years. He mentioned that a friend would be working for a business owner at another company. I asked, "Are they a collaborative leader or a boss?"

He responded, "They are a collaborative leader." I agreed, saying, "If he is a collaborative leader, then she will be working with him, not for him."

In another instance, I contracted an exceptionally young contractor to work on a property I acquired. During our conversation, he said, "I don't do that kind of work, but I have a team of people that work for me." Instantly, and without provocation, he restated his comment: "Well, they don't work for me; they work with me." At that moment, I thought, "He is my guy for this work." He is collaborative.

This is important as we have discussed how all the mentioned systems in the human organism work together. The same is true in business organizations, where the hierarchy collaborates with the "thinking-doing parts." Together...

Here is a normal EKG.

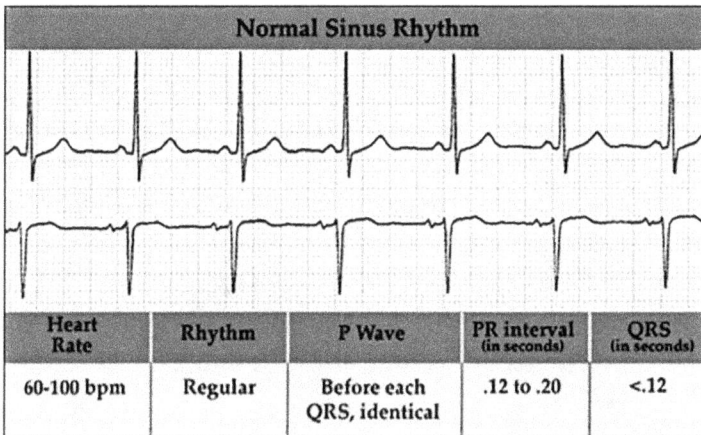

Heart Rate	Rhythm	P Wave	PR interval (in seconds)	QRS (in seconds)
60-100 bpm	Regular	Before each QRS, identical	.12 to .20	<.12

Figure 2 A.D.A.M.

Here we see what a normal EKG looks like. This image comes from a manual used to teach medical students how to interpret EKGs. In this case, the heart is functioning in a normal rhythm and at a steady rate within a prescribed timeframe—each vertical line represents a specific time interval and rate. This means there is work to be done; to meet customer demand, it must be accomplished within a certain timeframe and with the same quality we expect from our own hearts: consistently, autonomously, and reliably.

The heart, along with the lungs, is a critical element of existence, both in human organisms and in organizations. Therefore, the importance and regularity of the heart in business must be a top priority. I will conclude this section with a few real examples of what would be considered an abnormal EKG for a human, which may not be the case for a Business EKG, as we will explore.

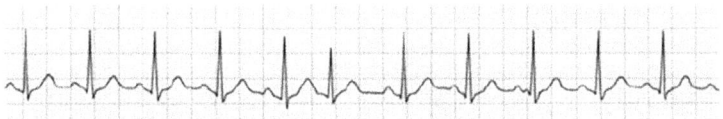

Figure 3 A.D.A.M.

Here we can see a pattern that exemplifies a high-performing team producing value in mostly equal increments. This is not typical cultural behavior in most organizations. Simply put, few companies can reach this crescendo and peak due to the "frozen layer" (stratified systems theory) and poor cultures that prevent people from understanding the real reasons they work, the impact they can have, and the commitment from top leadership.

Here is another Business EKG:

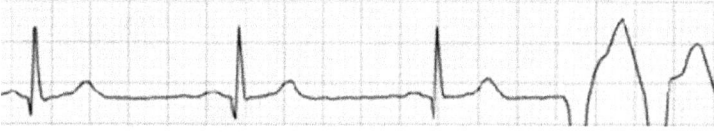

Figure 4 A.D.A.M.

This production/service team demonstrates a somewhat consistent pattern in their incremental work until disruptions occur. In many cases, when there is direct supervision and interruptions in demands, or when changes to requirements arise in the middle of development or production lines, we see disruptions in the value proposition. This inconsistency undermines predictability, leading to erratic performance. In these instances, quality suffers, which in turn raises customer concerns.

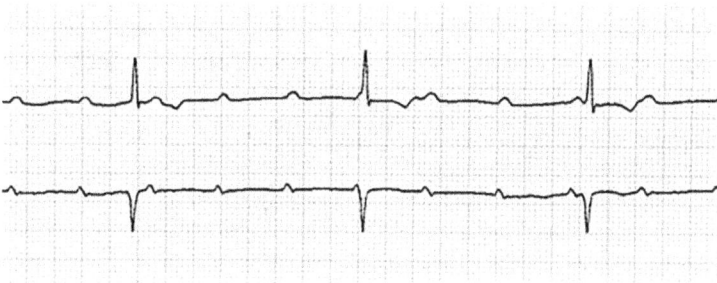

Figure 5 A.D.A.M.

Although there appears to be a consistent pattern in this Business EKG (of production), a closer look at the details of the increments reveals a very unpredictable pattern. None of the patterns repeat, and while there may be a visual sense of consistency, a closer examination shows that at the beginning of each cycle (the spike), there is no reliable start to the work, nor does it taper off toward the end of the increment as work is completed before moving on to the next set of customer requirements.

We could analyze EKGs for various heart-related patterns, including degrees of blockage (1st, 2nd, and 3rd degree), STEMI (heart attack), or any arrhythmias that can occur. Such analysis would yield more patterns that we could extrapolate into business scenarios, both positive and negative. The key point that Bittner makes is that with the Business EKG, we can clearly identify these patterns and predictively coach employees toward consistent, efficient, and high-quality products and services.

Bittner elegantly makes the case that future team performance can be anticipated by examining current performance to predict how a team might perform in the future. Additionally, this insight can be used to conduct team tune-ups once the information is known. With this approach, we can eliminate deadlines and reduce the stress on the system that often compromises quality. Conversely, you can predictively anticipate a timeframe for when the entire finished product or service can be implemented according to the established requirements, rate, and rhythm.

The last two GEMs are simple but perhaps the most powerful to use. First, because once you are trusted, you can influence anyone, meaning that everyone in your company can be influenced efficiently. Second, these GEMs will show you how to begin putting this knowledge into action.

First, understand that the greatest influence you can have when it comes to persuasion—only when you are trusted, as we discussed in "how to communicate"—is your ability to elicit an emotional state repeatedly.

There is a psychological technique used to associate a specific stimulus or trigger with a desired emotional or behavioral response. The idea behind this technique, called Mindset Markers, is similar to Pavlov's dog (stimulus-behavior) to keep the understanding simple. By consistently pairing a particular stimulus with a specific state or emotion, you can create an automatic association between the two.

This can then be utilized to elicit the desired response whenever the Mindset Marker is presented.

Overview of the Mindset Marker Technique

Establish a Desired State or Emotion: Start by identifying the emotional or behavioral state you want to associate with a specific trigger, known as a Mindset Marker. This could be a positive state like confidence or excitement, or a desired behavior, such as fostering innovation among employees.

Choose a Mindset Marker: Select a unique and easily recognizable stimulus that will be consistently paired with your desired state or emotion. This could take the form of a physical gesture, a specific word or phrase, a visual image, a sound, a touch, or even a particular handshake.

Create the Association: To establish the Mindset Marker, present the chosen stimulus simultaneously with the desired state or emotion.

For instance, if you want to associate confidence with a specific gesture, perform that gesture while experiencing or cultivating a strong sense of confidence. This technique can be applied to yourself, offering a quicker and easier way to embrace change rather than enduring it or resisting it.

Reinforce the Association: Repeat the pairing of the Mindset Marker with the desired state or emotion multiple times to strengthen the association. The more consistent and vivid the pairing, the more powerful the Mindset Marker will become.

Evoke the Response: Once the Mindset Marker is established, you can use it to elicit the desired response. Present the Mindset Marker on its own, allowing the associated state or emotion to be triggered automatically.

It's important to note that while the Mindset Marker can be a powerful technique, its ethical application is crucial. Persuasion engineering techniques should be used responsibly, with respect for others' autonomy and well-being. This brief description provides an overview of the Mindset Marker technique, which you can implement immediately as outlined, but remember that there are many nuances and variations to consider when applying it in practice.

Before we conclude with a last insight consider the following:

The "Thought Leadership Era" has brought a focus on expertise, innovation, and the influence of ideas as key drivers of value and competitive advantage. As this era evolves, it's likely we may see a transition into what could be called the "Empathy and Trust Era." This upcoming era would center around building deep, authentic relationships with customers, employees, and communities. Here's how it might look and why it makes sense as a natural progression:

1. Emphasis on Authentic Connection: While thought leadership emphasizes expertise, the next step will involve businesses showing that they understand and genuinely care about the needs, values, and emotions of their stakeholders. This may involve a greater focus on personalized experiences and ethical practices that align with consumer values.

2. Trust as a Key Asset: In a time when trust in institutions is at a premium, the next era may focus on businesses establishing themselves as not only thought leaders but also as trustworthy, values-driven entities. This will require transparency, integrity, and a commitment to social responsibility.

3. Collaborative and Community-Centric Models: Instead of positioning themselves solely as leaders or experts, companies will start creating collaborative platforms that empower communities. Rather than just telling, they'll be inviting—co-creating solutions and sharing credit with users, employees, and stakeholders.

4. Sustainable Impact: The "Empathy and Trust Era" may also entail a stronger push for environmental and social sustainability. Stakeholders will expect businesses to demonstrate measurable positive impacts on societal issues, making purpose and profitability more interconnected.

In summary, the next era could focus on deeper, more emotional engagement and trust-building, prioritizing transparency, co-creation, and responsibility over authority and expertise alone.

Lastly, *it is time to act*. As the "wise" Yoda once said, "Do or do not; there is no try." Now is the moment for you to begin your own organizational health journey.

The following technique may be familiar to you, but it will not work unless you employ it consistently. It encompasses much of what we have covered, with the most important aspect being the feedback loop.

The human organism makes incredible adjustments throughout its life, and business organizations must do the same.

PDCA—Plan-Do-Check-Act: This cycle is as simple as an action plan can be. (Mizuno, 1959) The key is to do something—act, move, begin. It has been said that nothing changes until something moves, a simple rephrasing of one of Isaac Newton's laws of physics.

Ultimately, we want results. Plan for them, take action, and then gather feedback; that's how you will know you're on track to achieve your goals. If you forge ahead without this feedback, you will certainly end up with a result, but it may not be the result you expected.

There are also other versions: OPDCA—Observe, PDSA—Study, etc.

All of these variations align with the idea that we should focus on what we want, not on what we do not want.

The key to success, in this case, is to act. One essential aspect of thriving in today's business environment is moving beyond mere contemplation and taking meaningful action. The Biological Audit (BA) Framework offers a straightforward and practical tool to assess the health of your organization, much like a medical check-up evaluates your physical well-being. This quick and easy assessment, designed with simplicity in mind, helps you gauge your business's vitality using a biological model presented throughout this book. It's an actionable step to ensure your organization is functioning optimally.

To get started, simply scan the QR code provided earlier for an introductory version of the BA Framework that you can complete in just 7 minutes.

Ultimately, expanding our awareness requires a willingness to step outside our comfort zones and explore new perspectives. While it may be challenging at first, with time, practice, and "good counsel" (which is different from legal counsel), we can learn to embrace a broader viewpoint and unlock new opportunities for growth and deeper, more powerful learning. This leads to outcomes that ultimately improve the bottom line.

A lack of action will certainly spell the demise of any business organization, whether through the slow, painful deterioration of its elements or a sudden collapse of its structure. The human experience has provided us with thousands of years of examples of how organizations can function effectively.

These GEMs, along with logical thinking systems, make a significant difference in our personal and professional progress. The call to action completes our preparation for your journey. This is about achieving the results we want for thriving businesses and engaged employees. In most cases, if these two factors exist, customers will be satisfied and happy with your products and services.

Using these thoughts, behaviors and methods combined will expedite our growth journeys and ultimately our success.

My best wishes to your health and your organization's health.

GRATITUDE

There are a host of people who have accompanied me on this journey of research, questions, answers, pre-reads, learnings, and observations. Without your support, this book would not have been possible.

Lee, thank you for tolerating my endless "head-in-a-book or on-a-call" moments. Daniel Pritchard, you read the first idea in an outline seven years ago and sent me questions that helped shape the book—thank you. Kevin, you have always been my biggest cheerleader, (like no one else.) You have believed in me and my work for over 30 years. You have my enduring love for that. Matt, Danny, Anthony, Greg, and Jimmy, when writer's block or life challenges arose you all brought levity and brightness, helping me see through the clouds. (Matt, thank you for looking out for Collin while he attended Princeton. Your support during some really dark times granted me the space to continue researching and writing). Joey, Moses, Sherrie, Steve, Anthony, and David, thank you for often listening to my rants on theories, thoughts, and ideas.

To my kids, Alexis and Collin, fresh out of school: you were my first editing eyes, and your pressure to "keep me a cool and relevant dad" profoundly influenced my writing. Thank you to my treasured list of pre-readers, who I pestered for months with emails, PDFs, images, covers, and multiple versions to get the style and flow of this book exactly right. My Aunt Sandra, who kept me grounded spiritually, thank you. I owe each of you a huge thanks and a big hug (perhaps dinner?). For those I have worked with, I owe you a debt of gratitude; there was so much to learn from all of you.

Thank you to the following for teaching and showing me these things:

Alexander Roesch:	you reignited my love for reading and taking 5 minutes to step outside in between meetings
Valerie Bryan RN:	empathy at work -through nursing
Lynn Whitley:	storytelling in education and training
Kristie Gitto RN:	the value of healthiness and honoring the human organism
Gov. Jim Hunt:	the power of influence
Attorney General Mike Easley:	the power of being strategic
Honorable Judge Wanda Bryant:	transparency, honesty and humility
Gwen Perry:	integrity
Paul Caldwell:	business management and the power of being entrepreneurial
Dr. John Murphy:	courage, equity, leadership
Trey Arey:	the power of challenging "you can't"
John LaValle:	Freedom

Maureen Kilkenny:	the meaning of service and support
Dr. Glen Mehltretter:	the absolute truth about hierarchies
Leo Logan:	balancing values and family with work
Dr. Elliott Jaques:	dedication, belief and persistence
MD, Ph.D.	engineering principles in action
Grover Melvin:	without fear
Dr. Ed Bell, Connie, Larry (Monnie, Penny, Dawn):	trust
Harry Virden:	patience, observation, avoiding micro-managing
Sandeep Ingale:	calmness in chaos
Captain Rip Dawson:	humility while constantly being the smartest person in the room (you taught me that I can still learn new skills in a matter of minutes) Familiarity – Breeds Confidence
Lisa Oborne:	authenticity, indifference vs. apathy, self- care and being me
Daniel Philipp:	thinking like a CEO and a consultant at the same time
Sec. George Sweat:	never compromise your "chosen" values
Dr. Ralph Taylor:	anything is possible
Anne Valentine RN:	the sanctity of life
Maria and Tony:	leaving the past behind

Joe S., Paula B. and Binesh S:	how to break barriers
Becky G, Arman K and Bill M:	the world is bigger than the six inches between my ears, no limits
Jay Gaertner, RN	in the middle of life's chaos, perspective and humor work miracles
Josh and Shane, MPT:	how resilient the human body can be …even as it ages, and the weekly book discussions and idea sharing.

These are just a few of the so many people with whom I have had the pleasure of working with and learning from. From technology to legal and law enforcement, from education to healthcare, from construction across America to roles in government; there has been a broad spectrum of careers and wonderful people along the way (too many to name and be able to write about in one lifetime) from which I have learned. I have nothing but gratitude for every position I have been able to serve in and the people that came along with it. My life is better, and I am smarter because of who I met; your uniqueness made a difference. Thank you, I am forever grateful.

REFERENCES

Womack, J. P., & Jones, D. T. (1996). *Lean Thinking: Banish Waste and Create Wealth in Your Corporation*. Simon and Schuster.

Leffingwell, D. (2017). *SAFe 4.0 Distilled: Applying the Scaled Agile Framework for Lean Software and Systems Engineering*. Addison-Wesley Professional.

Pyzdek, T., & Keller, P. A. (2014). *The Six Sigma Handbook*, Fourth Edition. McGraw-Hill Education.

Hayes, J. (2014). *The Theory and Practice of Change Management*. Palgrave Macmillan.

Adkins, L. (2010). *Coaching Agile Teams: A Companion for Scrum Masters, Agile Coaches, and Project Managers in Transition*. Addison-Wesley Professional.

Elliott Jacques, M. (1998). *Requisite Organization: A Total System for Effective Managerial Organization and Managerial Leadership for the 21st Century*. Cason Hall & Co Publishers.

Anderson, D. J. (2010). *Kanban: Successful Evolutionary Change for Your Technology Business*. Blue Hole Press.

Sanders, E. B. N., & Stappers, P. J. (2008). "Co-Creation and the New Landscapes of Design." *CoDesign*, 4(1), 5-18.

Imai, M. (1986). *Kaizen: The Key to Japan's Competitive Success.* McGraw-Hill.

Kolb, D. A. (2014). *Experiential Learning: Experience as the Source of Learning and Development.* FT Press.

Pink, D. H. (2009). *Drive: The Surprising Truth about What Motivates Us.* Riverhead Books.

Bennis, W. (1985). *Leaders: The Strategies for Taking Charge.* Harper & Row.

Collins, J. (2001). *Good to Great: Why Some Companies Make the Leap and Others Don't.* HarperCollins.

Drucker, P. F. (1994). "The Theory of the Business."

Harvard Business Review, 72(5), 95-104.

Gladwell, M. (2000). *The Tipping Point: How Little Things Can Make a Big Difference.* Little, Brown.

Bandler & Lavalle. (1996) *Persuasion Engineering*

Hammer, M., & Champy, J. (1993). *Reengineering the Corporation: A Manifesto for Business Revolution.* HarperCollins.

Heath, C., & Heath, D. (2010). *Switch: How to Change Things When Change Is Hard.* Crown Business.

Kotter, J. P. (1996). *Leading Change.* Harvard Business Press.

Lencioni, P. M. (2002). *The Five Dysfunctions Of A Team: A Leadership Fable.* John Wiley & Sons.

Peters, T. J., & Waterman, R. H. (1982). *In Search of Excellence: Lessons from America's Best-Run Companies.* Harper & Row.

Senge, P. M. (1990). *The Fifth Discipline: The Art and Practice of the Learning Organization.* Doubleday/ Currency.

Sinek, S. (2011). *Start with Why: How Great Leaders Inspire Everyone to Take Action.* Portfolio.

Carmichael, A. (2019). "Why We Freeze When We're Scared." *National Geographic.*

Retrieved from https://www.nationalgeographic.com/science/phenomena/2015/11/06/why-we-freeze-when-were-scared/.

A.D.A.M. Suite of Solutions, (2022). https:// medlineplus.gov/ encyclopedia.html, ECG, EKG, Ppt.

Langley, Gerald J. (2009). *"The Improvement Guide: A Practical Approach to Enhancing Organizational Performance."* Jossey-Bass

Martel, Laurence D. (2003) *"The Seven Secrets of Learning Revealed"* Cameo Publication